STORIED STUFF

Show and Tell for Grownups
Volume 1

Edited by Steve and Sharon Fiffer

CHRISTMAS LAKE PRESS

Published by Christmas Lake Press 2025
www.christmaslakecreative.com
Copyright © 2025 by Steve and Sharon Fiffer
ISBN 978-1-960865-29-8

All rights reserved. No part of this publication may be reproduced, stored in a retrieval system, or transmitted in any form, or by any means, electronic, mechanical, photocopying, recording, or otherwise without the prior permission in writing of the copyright holder, nor be otherwise circulated in any form or binding or cover other than the one with which it was originally published, without a similar condition being imposed on the subsequent publisher.

Interior layout by Daiana Marchesi

All profits from sales of this book will be donated to relief efforts for those affected by the 2025 California wildfires.

STORIED STUFF

Volume 1

Introduction

Five years ago we all were in a different place. A global pandemic kept us behind locked doors. And that's only if we were lucky enough to have the kind of work or the means to allow us to stay safely in our homes. Healthcare professionals, first responders, the deliverers of groceries, medicine and all the craft supplies that our new stay-at-home hobbies demanded or the pet food that our newly adopted dogs and cats required—those workers could not remain safely in isolation.

Remember how frantically we tried to stay busy, prevent panic, calm our children, contribute to our communities?

One of the ways we tried to cope was with Zoom. Remember life before Zoom? I do not. In addition to teaching classes, taking classes and holding meetings over Zoom, we also socialized with friends. Around the fourth week of our friends' Zoom get-together with five other couples, Steve had an idea to distract us all from our mourning and hand-wringing. Since everyone was cleaning and de-cluttering and rearranging like mad, why didn't everyone bring a treasured object from childhood and show the group, telling a story about how or why it was important to them?

That evening, one of our most successful Zooms, we all learned new things about each other. Steve, who had known Bill since kindergarten, never fully appreciated his fondness for model trains, never knew about Bill's relationship to his grandfather. Had we known Larry was a trophy-winning bowler? Had we ever taken the time to listen, really listen, to Pinky's memories of her beloved late brother as she showed his artwork?

After that evening, Steve suggested this could be an activity that would translate to the larger community, infinitely larger—the *internet* community. All we would need was a simple website and material. Our daughter and son-in-law could manage the website—storied-stuff.com—and we would find the material.

Some years ago I wrote an amateur sleuth series about a "picker" who was a treasure hunter and sentimental adopter of other peoples' cast-offs. Writing these Jane Wheel mysteries, all eight of which had the word "stuff" in the title, had convinced me that every bit of stuff we hang on to or are drawn to, tells a story.

The universal, after all, is found in the specific.

We spread the word about Storied Stuff through friends, friends of friends, and social media. We asked everyone we encountered if they, perhaps, had a story and an object to share.

Stories and photos appeared in our inbox, editor@storied-stuff.com. People, it seemed, could indeed look around their living space and find an object whose story resonated, whose story could be shared during this time of isolation and, for so many, grief and trauma. You'll note that many of the stories here, some of the earliest, reference Covid and its effects.

We posted two new entries weekly, with very little editing. Occasionally, we asked that the stories be more clearly tied to an object, but basically, although we are writers, teachers, and editors by profession, we refrained from tampering. We liked listening to someone share their story just the way they liked—and remembered.

Some 500 stories and "stuffs" later, we have arrived at our five-year anniversary.

Although Covid has not disappeared, it is more manageable. We now unlock our doors and venture out to see our friends and families. We travel again. The workplace has changed for most; the way we shop has been altered forever; and, I hope, that our appreciation for what teachers do all day in the classroom has been heightened.

But we still believe that stuff tells a story. Our story.

As I write this, preparing for the Storied Stuff book publication, with about half of the stories we've posted—the other half, Volume 2, will follow—it is January, 2025. The new year has turned, but instead of January bringing resolutions, high expectations, and hope, the month has brought the Santa Ana Winds to Southern California. Fire has destroyed Los Angeles neighborhoods—the homes, the community spaces, historic landmarks, churches and temples have been turned to ash. We do not yet have a final number for those who have lost their lives. As I type, the fires are not fully contained, we do not know what lies ahead.

What we do know is that is that so many have lost so much.

We believe in the power of storytelling—we won't presume to call it a "healing" power since everything is too new and raw to know what might heal—but there is power. And there is power in memory. Building back lives will take time and love and the commitment and resilience that we are seeing daily demonstrated during news interviews with direct victims of the fires. It will also take resources. Money.

Storied Stuff has always been a not-for-profit venture—no money has ever changed hands—but buying this book will require payment. With the cooperation of the estimable Christmas Lake Press, all profits from the sale of *Storied Stuff: Show and Tell for Grownups Volume I*, will go to organizations assisting those affected by the fires, both directly and indirectly, as well as other non-political not-for-profits. Here's to new beginnings, rebuilding, and making fresh memories. New stuff. New stories begin every day.

Sharon Fiffer, January 18, 2025

Publisher's Note

Because these are personal essays, each author's individual style—including punctuation, capitalization, the placement of commas, the use of dashes, and the treatment of numbers—has been retained.

Contributors in Order of Appearance

Gabi Coatsworth | Adrienne Gallagher | Esther Cohen | Jim Dorr | Beth Inlander | Arnie Kanter | Evalynne Gould Elias | Francie Arenson Dickman | Jack Hertz | Jack Doppelt | Junior Burke | Noelle Allen | Laura B. Becker | Nancy O'Brien Dorr | Phil Kirschbaum | Judy Kassouf Cummings | Carol Bobrow | James Finn Garner | Cathy Kinard | Kathryn L. Kaplan | Judi Geake | Joe Garber | Larry Gritton | Susie Butterfield | Julie Cowan | Lillian Dailey | Robert Bissell | Barbara Walter Hetler | Jenny Klein | Dennis Baron | Lisa Hart | Keir Graff | Marylou DiPietro | George Kovac | Marilyn Kochman | Chuck Frank | Patricia Adelstein | Chuck Brown | Nan Doyal | Manny Brown | Nancy Hepner Goodman | Mary Loretta Kelly | N. G. Haiduck | Peggy Heitman | Candice Glicken | Pam Gassel | Elaine Johnson | Joni Blecher | Mary B. Hansen | Susan Grout | Kathy Brant | William Anthony | Liza Blue | Lynn Bodnar | Pat Hitchens | Pat Kreger | Keith Kretchmer | Thomas G. Fiffer | Laurie Kahn | Tuni Deignan | Annette Gendler | Joanna Clapps Herman | Mark Larson | Kathleen Caprario-Ulrich | Ina Chadwick | Suzanne Guess | Judy Iacuzzi | Lisa Lauren | Fred Karger | Valerie Kretchmer | Fred Gants | Bob Kaufman | Robert J. Elisberg | Allyson Dykhuizen | Josh Kaplan | Betsy Lackey | Elizabeth Drucker | Jean Harned Boyle | Abigail Brooks | Jim Dodds | Bill Durden | Robert Jordan | Mike Conklin | Sally deVincentis | Larry Cohan | Becca Taylor Gay | Patricia Merritt Lear | Bobbie Calhoun | Jim Cunningham | Peggy Wagner Kimble | Sue Gano | Carol Kanter | Paula Beardell Krieg | Christine Goodwin | Barbara Huffman | Mary Campbell | Bonny Howe | Judy Frank Frohlich | Karen Fulks | Reed Ide | Lester Jacobson | Melissa Hunt | Jean Diamond | David Inlander | Ken Hersh | Linda Gartz | Sharon Fiffer | Steve Fiffer

Storied Stuff

GABI COATSWORTH

My father was stranded in England after World War II. So, he wasn't an immigrant, exactly—he hadn't made a plan to leave Poland for better things. I suppose, technically, he was a refugee.

What he *had* done, before the world went to war, was to leave his homeland in 1938 to work in the Polish consulate in Toulouse, France, for a year. He was an agricultural economist, and at 25, had no ties to prevent him from going.

While he was there, he bought his mother a porcelain bottle of *Violettes de Toulouse* perfume, shaped like a tiny watering can, intending to give it to her when he returned home. But when Hitler marched into Poland, my father joined many of his compatriots who were living and working in France to form a Polish Army. They fought the Germans side by side with the French, only to find themselves backed up against the English Channel at Dunkerque, praying for a miracle.

They got one. Almost everyone was rescued and delivered to England by a flotilla of small fishing boats, dinghies, and yachts, which volunteered when the troopships couldn't manage alone. My father arrived on the south coast—with only the uniform he stood up in and the perfume for his mother—to be put on a train along with his comrades, bound for the north of England, where he trained as a paratrooper.

At the end of the war, Polish soldiers in Britain were offered a free (one-way) ticket to Poland, now an officially Communist country. My father had met my English mother by then, and fallen in love. He was faced with a heartrending decision. To travel back to his family

—parents, siblings and cousins—whom he hadn't seen for six years, in the knowledge that the Polish Government would be unlikely to let him leave if he did. Or to stay in Britain until the Communists left.

He decided to stay in Britain. It wasn't easy. His homeland now had a new name—the People's Republic of Poland, and his old consular passport was of no use. After he married my mother, he applied for a British passport, hoping this might let him visit Poland, but the British wouldn't grant him one.

My father became a stateless person and he died sixteen years later, without a country and without seeing his mother again. When I traveled to Poland at the age of ten, I delivered the *Violettes de Toulouse* to her, not understanding the significance of her tears until many years later. And when I returned again to see the family in 2018, my cousins presented me with the bottle I'd last seen in 1960.

It's empty now, but that little watering can is full of the scent of history.

JANUARY MINUTES *A.L.I.S.A.*

The meeting was called to order 6:50 P.M. by Leslie on 1-13-59.

The minutes were read by Leslie.

Dad commented that the "minutes stink in spades".

OLD BUSINESS:
Dad said that the children "owe" making of one supper from Christmas vacation. They promised to make this up.

Dad brought up the fact that the children should try earning money on the outside. Adrienne mentioned her experience with the lemonade stand - Everyone laughed - Adrienne cried. Leslie stated that she earned some money baby-sitting. No conclusion.

NEW BUSINESS:
Children stated they wanted to go to the circus. If everything is okay, we will go.

There was discussion regarding study methods and bed-time during finals. If person studies diligently from the time of arrival from school, he should be permitted to stay up to finish study before exams.

Children stated that plans for weekend should be decided by individuals. Plans must be "subject to parental approval". This is to be discussed further at next meeting.

Adrienne complained regarding Leslie's knocking at door and then entering without waiting for permission. It was decided that Leslie should knock at bathroom door and wait for permission.

Everyone is to use their own hair-brush. The hair-brush in the bathroom may be used by anyone as long as it is used in the bathroom and not removed therefrom.

Meeting adjourned 7:28 P.M.

Submitted by Irene P.

ADRIENNE GALLAGHER

When I was seven, my family started having family meetings. We took turns running the meetings and being the secretary, following *Robert's Rules of Order*, a book my parents thought was vital to our success in life.

Here's an excerpt from a meeting of the A.L.I.S.A. Club (our initials) on July 10, 1958. My older sister was the secretary.

OLD BUSINESS: Steve said he should have a raise. We discussed. Mommy made the motion and Stephen didn't get a raise. Les said the same thing. We discussed. Daddy made the motion. (It was defeated.) Ade said she wanted to go to bed later to catch lightning bugs. No.

NEW BUSINESS: I said I wanted to wear lipstick every day in the summer. No, of course not. Mommy made the motion. It was tied. Will be carried until the next meeting.

The meetings continued. Can I quit piano? Can we go to bed later? Where should we go on vacation? Can we go to the circus? Can the person who knocks on the bathroom door wait before entering? This last one request actually got some traction. And also, we did agree to go to the circus. But generally, according to the meeting notes, there could be discussion, "but no arguments will be tolerated."

On February 9, 1960, my brother made a motion to stop having meetings. Motion defeated.

ESTHER COHEN

I've been foraging and gathering for as long as I can remember random irrational objects, objects that evoke. My mother started the process when I was very young – say six or seven. She was born in Grand Forks, North Dakota, and in one of those small stories that makes a life, she found herself married and living in a small factory town called Ansonia, where I was born. She loved to drive, claimed to have been driving since she turned 12. Grand Forks, she said, was not a place with traffic.

She would drive often, and I would accompany her. She liked thrift stores especially, although the world she lived in was all about NEW.

Over the years I've collected a range of things starting with umbrella handles, but I have consistently searched for good words, and interesting handwriting. I would buy postcards for the messages, and for the shape of the letters of the strangers who wrote them. I collected many postcards where the writer wrote, "We Are Here," with a big black X on a picture of a motel, on a lake or waterfall. A week ago at a flea market in East Durham, New York, I found a postcard that said, "Dear Joan, You Will Never Hear from Me Again." The writer, named Alan, did not say why.

One of my all-time favorites is a long box I've been carrying around for years. For the handwriting and, of course, the subject: Box Old Envelopes, carefully handwritten.

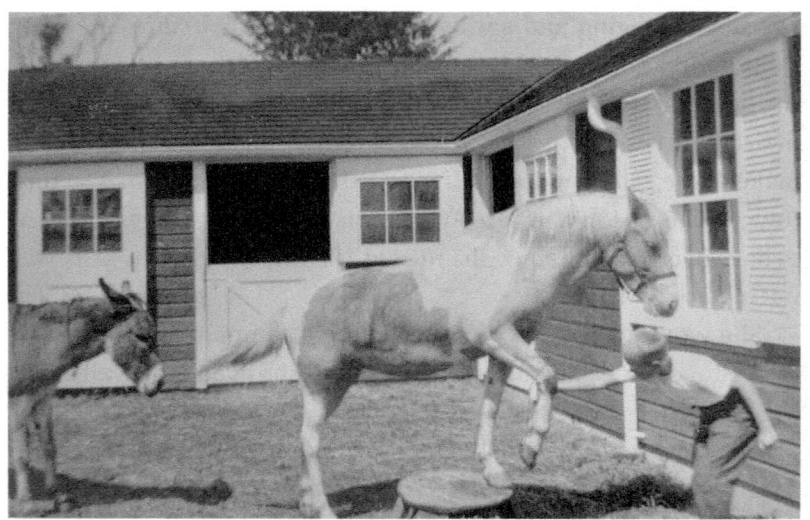

JIM DORR

When I was eight, I devoured every adventure book about animals I could find. Authors Walter Farley, Jim Kjelgaard and, especially, Marguerite Henry were favorites.

In August, 1953, my parents and I came to Chicago from our home in Dubuque, Iowa, for a weekend of Cubs games. I asked if we could drive by Marguerite Henry's home in west suburban Wayne, thinking I might see Misty of Chincoteague or Brighty of the Grand Canyon. Driving through Wayne, we asked a lady on a horse for directions to Marguerite Henry's house. To our surprise, she replied: "I am Marguerite Henry," and invited us to her home.

That day was magic. She took me for a ride on Friday, her Morgan horse. We talked about her books; she was very interested in learning what I liked best about them. She wanted me to know that they were based on true characters and events. We shared ice cream and cake left over from a birthday party for Misty that 100 children had attended. I shook hooves with Misty while Brighty looked on. And Ms. Henry autographed *Born to Trot*.

I still have that book, plus *Misty, Sea Star, Justin Morgan, King of the Wind*, and *Brighty*. I also have our subsequent correspondence. She liked the hotpads I sent her for Christmas and the picture of Brighty seeming to exit the front door of her house. She sent a letter received in December, 1953, from the man who managed the tourist camp called Wyleys and who knew the real Brighty before he died 31 years before. He thought *Brighty* had "plenty of pep" and confirmed many of the events, including the involvement of the gold watch.

That should be intriguing enough to make you want to read the book, even if you are an adult.

BETH INLANDER

I'm an avid reader, nurtured by my mother's love for books, which she imparted to me in so many ways. I recited nursery rhymes she read to me by 18 months. Her weekly trips to Chicago's Loop invariably resulted in the gift of a Golden Book. My bedroom was decorated with pictures of fairy tale characters framed by red duct tape. At eight, I was thrilled when we moved to a house where I could sneak into my closet and read with a flashlight late into the night.

Nothing captivated me more than the books from my mother's childhood, especially *The Patchwork Girl of Oz*, by L. Frank Baum. My parents read it aloud to my brother and me on our annual summer road trip. What a fantastical quest through Oz with Ojo the Unlucky accompanied by Scraps, the crazy quilt Patchwork Girl; and Bungle, the glass cat.

Flash forward, and I delighted in reading the same book to my children, Michael and Amy, so they, too, could be enchanted by the quest to bring Ojo's beloved Unc Nunky and the Crooked Magician's wife back to life after a tragic accident turned them to marble!

Now, sequestered at home during the pandemic, my favorite time of day is reading over Zoom to my grandsons, Max and James. After making our way through some short chapter books, we began [The Patchwork Girl of Oz](). While sharing the same adventure with a fourth generation of our family, I hear my mom's familiar voice drifting across our motel room and feel the weight of my kids on my lap as I read to them. Although summer trips and close contact aren't possible in these strange times, the constant of sharing this story uplifts me.

ARNIE KANTER

The inside cover of my red, leatherette autograph book reads, in a child's printing, "Dec 9, 1950 Arnold Kanter eight years old 3B."

It was an open secret to baseball nuts my age back then that teams visiting Chicago to play the White Sox, with one exception, stayed at the Del Prado Hotel in Hyde Park. The exception was the Cleveland Indians, the only American League team with a Negro ball player, Larry Doby. Since the Del Prado would not admit Doby, the Indians all stayed downtown. I loved the Indians for that.

But that racial prejudice never stopped a large flock of kids from surrounding the hotel, autograph books in hand, accosting other teams' players as they entered or left. Occasionally, a kid would try sneaking into the hotel lobby, but the bellmen would always catch him and deposit him back outside.

I was the only kid allowed inside. Friends of our family ran the lobby cigar/newsstand, which was visited by virtually every player. Enthroned behind that stand with our family friend, I sat with my red leatherette autograph book.

I scored autographs from famous ballplayers, including Joe DiMaggio, Bob Feller and Mickey Mantle. But my favorite, written in a shaky hand, reads, "With best wishes for a long and happy live (sic) is the wish." The person signing it was Cornelius McGillicuddy, better known as Connie Mack, then 88-years-old. Mack was a light-hitting catcher (5 home runs in 11 seasons), but his 3731 wins as a manager are almost 1000 more than any other manager in history.

What most endears Mack to me, though, is his 3948 losses, 1700 more than his nearest competitor. As a lifelong Cubs fan, I treasure Mack's autograph as evidence that you can lose a lot and still live, long and happy.

Storied Stuff

EVALYNNE GOULD ELIAS

I don't remember how or when we kids got our red wagon. It seemed that we always had it. This was in the mid-1950s, and having a Radio Flyer was a sort of staple of childhood. You could use it for just about anything. But what I remember most was using it to do the kind of errands that made me feel grown up and important.

There was a little grocery store half a block from our house in Bordentown, NJ. This was before there were any supermarkets near our town. It was owned by Italian immigrants, Jimmy Granata and his mother. My mother would call Jimmy with a list and then send me to pick up the groceries.

She never gave me money. I would walk down to Jimmy's with my wagon, and he would always ask me: "Pay now or pay later?" The answer was always the same: "Pay later." Then he'd load up the Red Flyer, and I'd bring them back home.

(An aside: Jimmy was also a bookie. Often while I was waiting for my groceries, Jimmy would be on the phone speaking in barely disguised code: "So you'd like an order of four bananas and you'll pick up at six?")

As I grew older I forgot all about the wagon. When it came time for me to sell my parents' home a few years ago, I learned that they didn't throw out *anything*. There in a basement corner, rusted and alone, stood my Radio Flyer. I knew that this was not going to be discarded into the trash heap of long lost flotsam and jetsam my parents had tucked away. This was going to be rescued and resurrected. I brought it to my home in Kentucky, where, I admit, for several years it sat forgotten in my own basement.

One of the positive side effects of this Covid quarantine is that it gives us time to think to discover anew long forgotten projects. Out came that old Radio Flyer to be restored. It now sits on my deck, bejeweled with potted herbs. And whenever I sit on my deck or go out to cut some herbs, I can't help but remember: "Pay now, or pay later?"

FRANCIE ARENSON DICKMAN

I loved, and will always love, Snoopy. My Snoopy, stuffed though he was, had a wardrobe. A bathing suit, in case he felt like a swim. Overalls, for casual. Tennis togs with a visor, so the sun didn't interfere with his overhead. An umbrella, in case it rained. He also had a tuxedo, which he wore on Saturdays to host the *Snoopy Talk Show*, an unscripted affair during which Snoopy chatted with Woodstock and other A- and B-list stuffed animals. I was showrunner; getting animals from the green room, pressing play on the cassette recorder, editing afterwards, forcing my brother to listen.

As beloved as Snoopy himself, was his "stuff." The miniature "Peanuts" notebooks, pencil sets and memo pads which were sold uptown at Chestnut Court and which I collected and coveted. But never used. They were precious. They were possibility.

That it all—the obsession with a dog who, in comic strip or imagination, personified and embodied every kind of character including author, and that he had his own line of notebooks and pens, the stuff of writers—was an indication of who I was and what I liked to do, never crossed my mind.

Until yesterday, when I was driving along, listening to Ann Patchett read her essay, *Snoopy Taught Me How To Be a Writer*. "Me too, me too," I wanted to scream. "Thank you," I wanted to say, for the insight. All these years, I assumed my infatuation with Snoopy stemmed from wanting to have a dog. Maybe, too, it stemmed from wanting to be a writer.

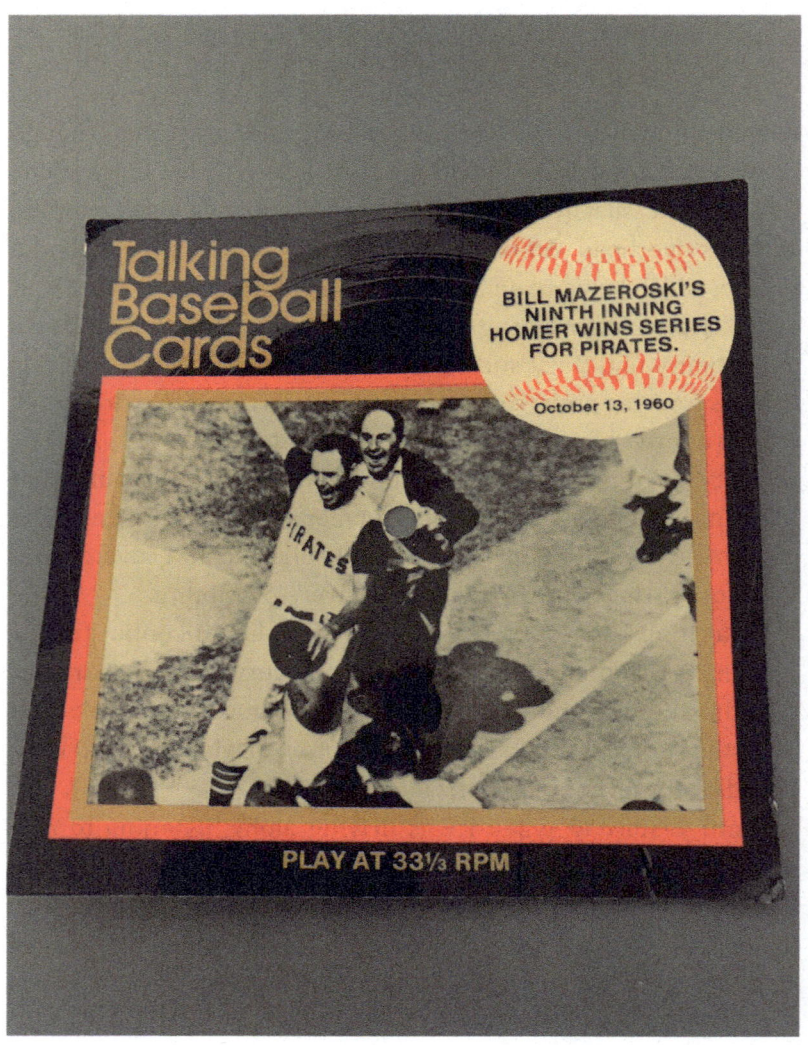

JACK HERTZ

I was at Forbes Field, home of the Pittsburgh Pirates, on October 13, 1960, but not at 3:36 PM, when Bill Mazeroski hit his home run off of the NY Yankees' Ralph Terry in the bottom of the ninth inning to win the 1960 World Series—the only time a walk-off homer has won a Game 7 in baseball history. Thanks to the retrieval of rare tv footage, you can now watch the entire game on YouTube. But until recently, the pictured recording was all I had to relive that grand day in the life of an eleven-year-old boy.

The Yankees, had knotted the game 9 to 9 in the top of the ninth. Mazeroski, who had hit a mere 11 homers during the regular season, led off the bottom of the inning.

My recording features Hall of Fame broadcaster Chuck Thompson's historic call: "Here's the swing, there's a high fly ball going deep to left, this may do it, back to the wall goes Berra, it is over the fence—home run, the Pirates win!!!"

Now how could I have been in the stadium, but not have seen the game? My late, beloved father, Joe Hertz, worked for Allegheny Cigarette Service. His job, that day, was to fill the twenty-seven cigarette machines in the stadium before the game. He took me with him, as he had done many times before. He was such a highly principled man, that he thought it was wrong to remain at the park without a ticket. So we left before the game started and listened on the radio.

Of course, hearing the call wasn't the same as being there to see THE GREATEST HOME RUN IN BASEBALL HISTORY. I think my dad understood. That night he loaded the family into the DeSoto and took us downtown to the rally for the champs.

While I still have the recording (as well as Maz's rookie card and a signed ball), the Hall of Famer himself has not been as sentimental. In 2013, he put the jersey he was wearing when he hit the homer up at auction. It sold for $632,500.

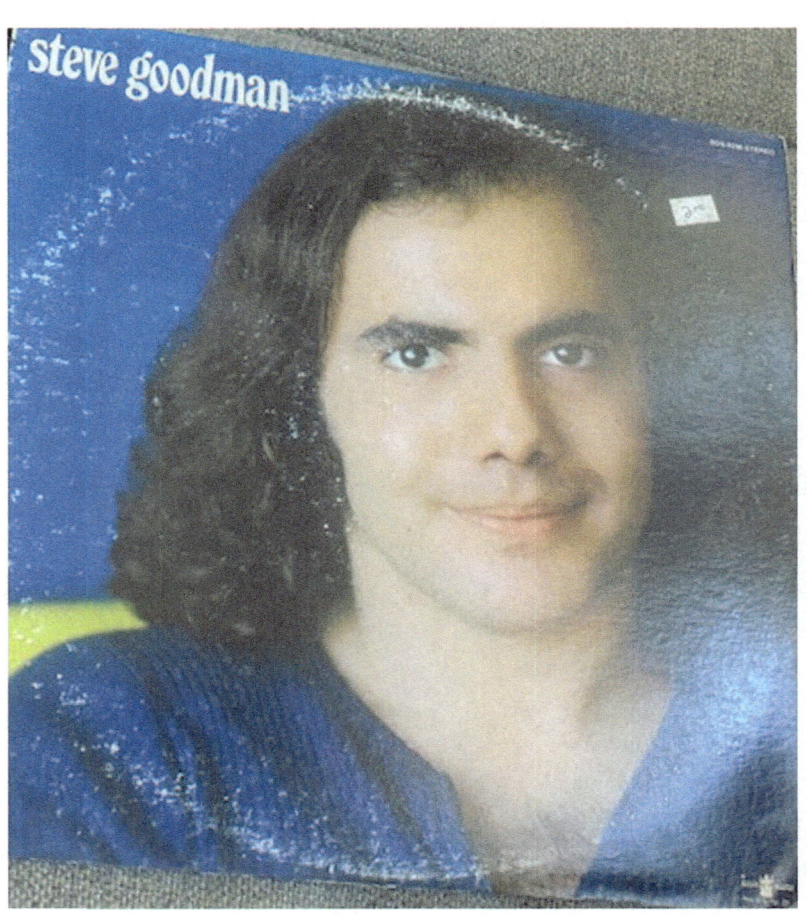

JACK DOPPELT

I bought this album used for $2.

I didn't own a stereo until freshman year in college, when some of my high school buddies hitchhiked from Chicago to Grinnell to present me with one. My family had no stereo or record player, so growing up, I played no albums or 45s. I spent most of my time at home, watching TV with my parents. Otherwise, I listened to music on AM radio.

The stereo gift and the weekend sojourn to Grinnell were surprises rendered insignificant by the happenstance delivery method that accompanied the gift and my friends. The guy who picked up my hitchhiking buddies was Steve Goodman, for us one of the most exhilarating performers we hitched our wagons to. I'm told my buddies got into the car and Goodman asked where they were headed. They said Grinnell and he said, "What a coincidence, I'm playing at Grinnell tonight."

The gig was in an intimate setting. At one point Goodman said, "Apparently somebody here has a birthday. Why don't we give that person a chance for a request." I asked for *I'm My Own Grandpaw*, a goofball song from the '40s that Goodman sang with relish.

The Goodman connection does not end there. When I met Margie—who would become my wife—our first date was to go to Milwaukee Summerfest because they were featuring Steve. We fell in love that day, of course.

Early the following fall, on Sept. 24, 1984, the Cubs clinched their first post-season opportunity since 1945. Goodman, possibly the Cubs' most enduring fan, didn't get a chance to celebrate. Twelve years into his bout with leukemia, he died four days before the Cubs clinched. He had written the "Go Cubs Go" anthem and "A Dying Cub Fan's Last Request," which he'd been singing since 1981.

At the time, I was working at WBBM Newsradio and was responsible a few months later for writing a year-ender about Goodman.

Fast forward to children. We have two. A couple of years ago, Noah, the younger, and I decided to create a game together. It's evolved into Lines n' Lyrix, an online game that riffs off of song lines. From the lyrics on the screen, you guess the name of the song, who's known for singing it and who wrote it. We release five questions online a day. You'll find I'm *My Own Grandpaw* in the country edition. Check out Q. 4 when you play.

As a bonus, you can find five Goodman tunes buried in various editions. You'll have to play to unearth them. It's worth it. Where else would you find, "Dealin' card games with the old men in the club car, penny a point ain't no one keepin' score."

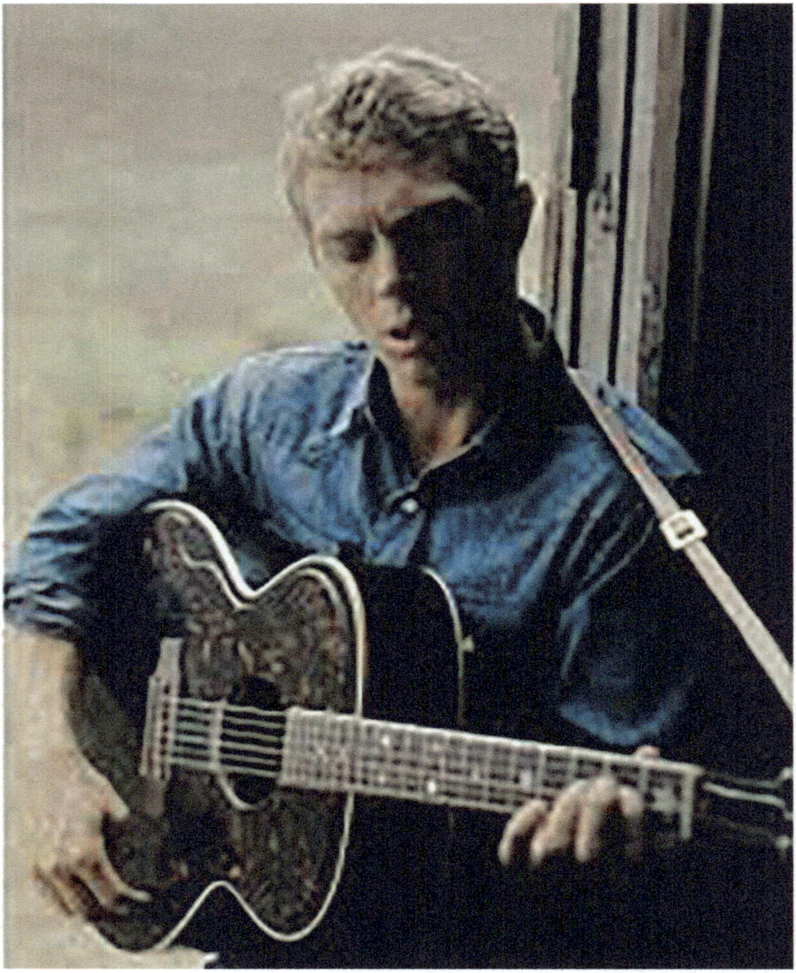

JUNIOR BURKE

At nineteen, I, who did not read music, who had capriciously left my one and only guitar lesson never to return, decided to be a songwriter.

I contacted a fellow I knew who owned an area music store and asked if he could help me get my hands on a Gibson Everly Brothers.

The only one I'd ever glimpsed was worn by Steve McQueen, playacting at playing guitar in the film *Baby, the Rain Must Fall*. I'd never even seen the Everly Brothers wearing one. But I thought it was the most beautiful instrument, black with over-sized double tortoise-shell pick guards and gleaming white five-pointed stars adorning several of the frets.

The storeowner got back to me and said yes, he could order one, and we worked out a deal. While most young songwriters at that time were coming to songwriting via folk music, I was coming from Chuck Berry and Buddy Holly. This was the guitar I wanted because, although acoustic, it looked like rock n' roll.

It didn't arrive for several months. What I didn't know until later was that Gibson was phasing this model out, having sold but a few hundred in going on ten years. But it was the guitar for me. Within a week I'd written two songs on it. Thankfully, it's still with me, on its stand in the living room, half a century old. A few scuffs and scratches and suitably mellow.

Storied Stuff

NOELLE ALLEN

I was born in the Mormon church and acquired all the baggage that comes from an institution with clear gender expectations. My main worth was as a future mother. My main role was to learn how to be a good wife, how to raise my children in God's ways, and how to make a home where my family would be safe from the dangers of the world.

For a few years in my childhood, I got to see a different way to live. We still went to church. We still feared the world and its dangers. But my mother became the breadwinner and my father became the homemaker.

In my memory, this period of time is when both of my parents were happiest. My dad loved to cook. My mom enjoyed having professional relationships with other adults. My dad was good at nurturing. My mom was good at being capable and smart.

In general, Mormon women avoid working outside the home. If circumstances require them to work for a paycheck, they live with the guilt that they're not fulfilling their divine duties. Not my mom. I have no memories of her feeling conflicted about working. She didn't apologize for being absent so much. She even took opportunities to be absent more, such as taking evening classes for fun. These included a jewelry making class, where she made me this turtle pendant for my birthday.

My mom showed me that we are all free to choose what will make us happiest.

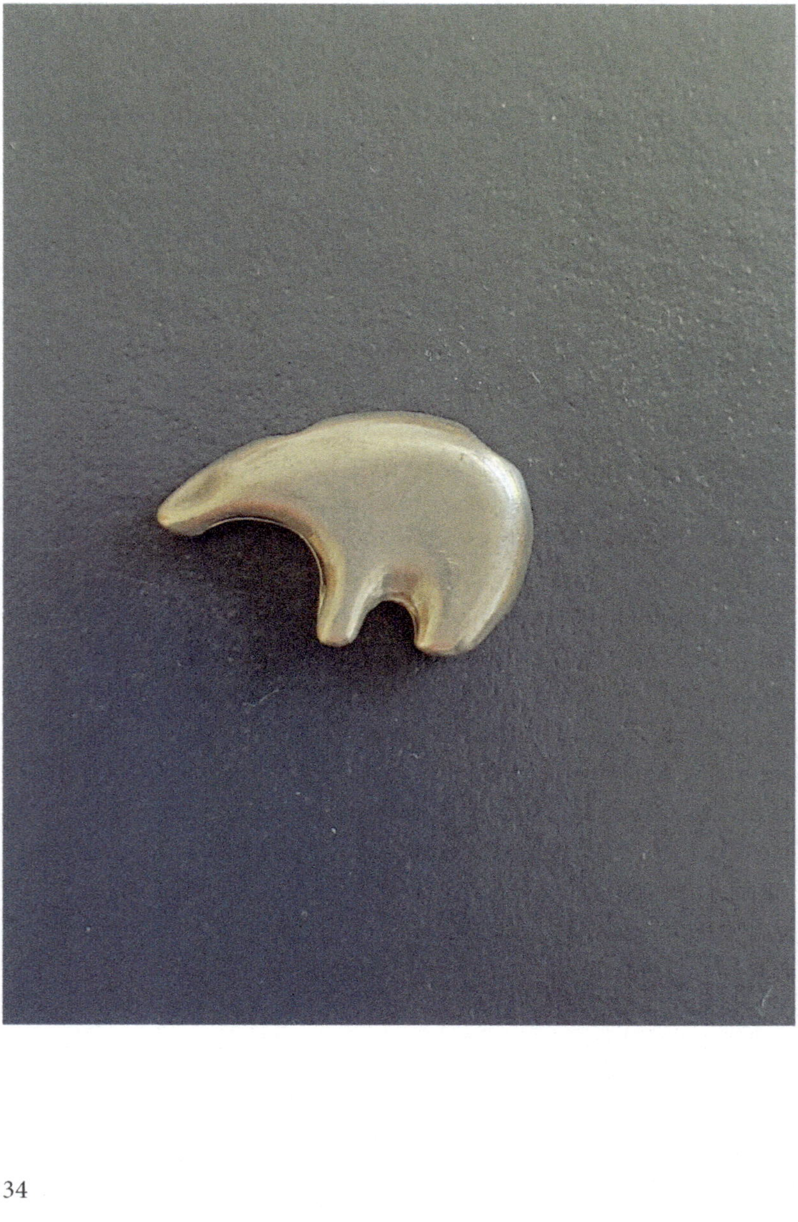

LAURA B. BECKER

Being the first in my family to pursue doctoral work, I never truly understood how my parents viewed this endeavor. Even though both of my parents, Maxine and Norman, valued education, they were never afforded the opportunity that I was able to undertake.

Because of circumstances of marrying and moving as I began writing the dissertation, and then having a child, and subsequently divorcing, my path to completion of the research and writing had many interruptions. Consequently, the delay in completing and defending my dissertation was significant.

As one might imagine, during this time of tumult, I had great doubts about my abilities to design and carry out the experiments, and especially to write clearly about the results and the significance of the work. I had great support from my academic advisors and colleagues, but even more important was the emotional support I had from my parents.

Upon the completion of the dissertation defense, my parents sponsored a celebration attended by my dissertation committee, friends, colleagues, and most importantly, my daughter. After the celebration, my parents gave me a precious gift that I cherish to this day: a Navaho sterling silver bear fetish with the following note: "This bear fetish is a symbol of power and courage, qualities that we have always known you to possess. Your perseverance allowed you to come to this special and important day."

When I wear it around my neck and when I think of the bear fetish, I can feel not only the Navaho symbolism, but also the great strength and support of my parents. For this I am forever grateful.

Storied Stuff

NANCY O'BRIEN DORR

Have you ever wondered about degrees of separation? Like, does a butterfly in Japan flapping its wings cause a gentle breeze at 42nd and Broadway in New York? How about this story:

In the mid '70s, I bought a Native American necklace at Saks Fifth Avenue for my mother's birthday. She loved jewelry, especially jewelry she could wear with her beautiful sterling silver earrings when vacationing in the West. She loved the necklace!

When my youngest sister Kate was to be married in 1981 in Lincoln, NE, another sister asked Mother if she could wear it to the wedding. Mother acquiesced, with trepidation. No one told me this. Several years later, Mother asked me if there might be another necklace like the one I gave her. I thought this was a strange question, but thought nothing more.

Meanwhile, the now married sister had moved to Chicago, where her husband completed his medical internship. Shortly before they moved to Utah in 1985, my sister and husband were visiting the apartment of a fellow medical student. After exiting the restroom adjacent to the master bedroom, Kate saw a wall covered in her host's jewelry collection. Liking jewelry runs in the family, so Kate found herself examining the collection. Imagine her surprise when she discovered the necklace, identical to the one I had given our mother, and the one worn to her wedding by another sister.

When Kate asked her hostess where she had gotten the necklace, the hostess replied that sometime in the early '80s, she had found it in the gutter of a downtown Lincoln, NE, street near a large hotel, where I now know my sister had lost it years before. The necklace is now one of my prized possessions.

Did you feel a breath of air?

Storied Stuff

PHIL KIRSCHBAUM

It was my first job interview after college. My mom and dad wanted me to be prepared. They were afraid that after four years of living as a hippie and protesting the war in Vietnam, nothing had prepared me for a job interview. So here was their three-step plan:

Step #1. Haircut. That, my mom entrusted to her hair stylist Maestro Gerhardt. The Maestro's first words to me were "You vill get ze shag cut."

Step #2. Suit. That my dad entrusted to Johnny Amodei at Denis Menswear in Skokie.

Step #3. Their graduation gift: A gold necklace with my "Zodiac Sign" - a nod to my hippie lifestyle and the Broadway play *Hair*. A compromise from Irv and Flo.

Armed with my shag haircut, my suit, and my necklace, I ventured downtown to begin this new chapter of my life. Walking along Michigan Avenue to my interview in Chicago's South Loop, I stopped to look at my reflection in a store window. I was stunned by what I saw. I didn't recognize this person. It seemed I had abandoned everything that was important to me.

Just beyond the image of myself in the window, I saw a group of high school kids pointing at me. I could see and hear them laughing at me. One of the kids said, "Check out this dude." That was followed by a round of uproarious laughter from his friends.

I wanted to die. I wanted to turn around and yell to the kids: "This isn't me!"

I did, however, get the job.

I haven't worn the necklace in over 40 years. I keep it in a box of treasured, sacred objects from my life. Maybe it's still bringing me good luck.

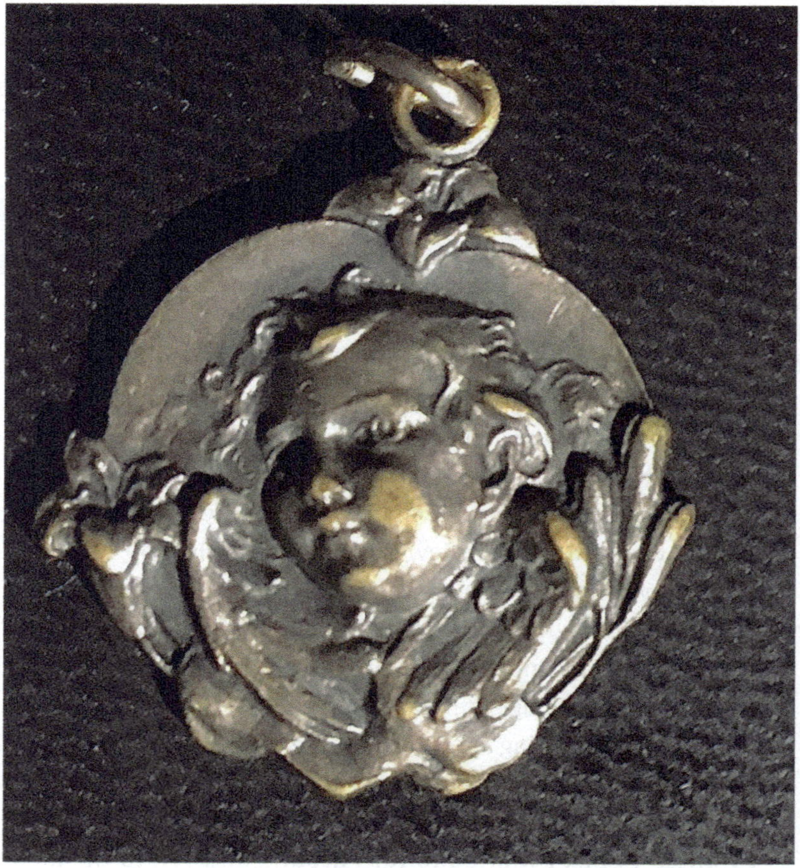

JUDY KASSOUF CUMMINGS

For the dead and the living, we must bear witness.
— Elie Wiesel

In sixth grade, I was given the assignment to interview an elderly person. Wondering whom to ask, I turned to Mom, who suggested that I interview her friend Dorothy's husband. My mother knew he had a story to tell.

Mom was Lebanese; Dorothy was Jewish. Yet a firmer friendship couldn't be found, one born of differences and mutual respect. Nervously, I crafted questions while Mom spoke with her friend.

From the moment we arrived, the family treated us graciously. As I took out my questions, Mr. Blumenthal rolled up his shirt sleeve to reveal a sequence of numbers tattooed on his arm.

"Do you know what these represent?" he asked.

"Yes," I replied. "You have been in the camps."

"You know..." he stated, "but now, I will tell you what you do not know."

Mr. Blumenthal began matter-of-factly to recount his time in a German concentration camp, Buchenwald. He told me of his arrival by train and how he was forced to strip naked, then clubbed repeatedly by a gauntlet of soldiers as he ran between them to enter the iron gates.

"Many died before arriving," he said. "All this was done to demoralize us. Once inside, we read the inscription: 'Jedem das Sein,' or *To Each His Own*.

He described living conditions. "We received little to eat, some soup and dry bread. It was really more like lukewarm water - few vegetables and barely any meat. If we came across a sliver of meat, we'd share it with those who were starving."

He went on to say that because water was so scarce, his most precious possession was a spoon. "Whenever it rained, we'd take turns holding the spoon, catching droplets to drink."

He paused, then continued, "In the camp we worked from morning until night, dropping from exhaustion, malnutrition, or illness." He said that the smell of death was everywhere.

More than 56,000 people perished at Buchenwald. Attempts to rebel or escape resulted in a ticket to death. Yet, on April 11, 1945, anticipating their liberation, the prisoners stormed the watchtowers, taking control. Later that day, the 6th Armored Division helped free more than 21,000 people.

After my visit, I felt a sense of the sacred.

Whereas today some try to hide the world's injustices from children, the "Greatest Generation" understood that doing so would rob young minds of a balanced perspective, rendering them historically illiterate and ill-prepared for adulthood.

As I turned to leave, Dorothy handed me a small medal saying, "Remember."

The medal replicates an angel with outstretched wings that sits atop St. Paul's Cathedral in London. While having been pummeled during WW2, St. Paul's escaped major damage. The bells still ring out. They chimed at the liberation of Paris in 1944 and sounded again in 1945 to mark the end of war in Europe.

Just as Mr. Blumenthal escaped death, St. Paul's escaped devastation. And this little medal reminds me of our great duty to protect humanity by bearing witness, fighting injustice, and proclaiming truth.

Storied Stuff

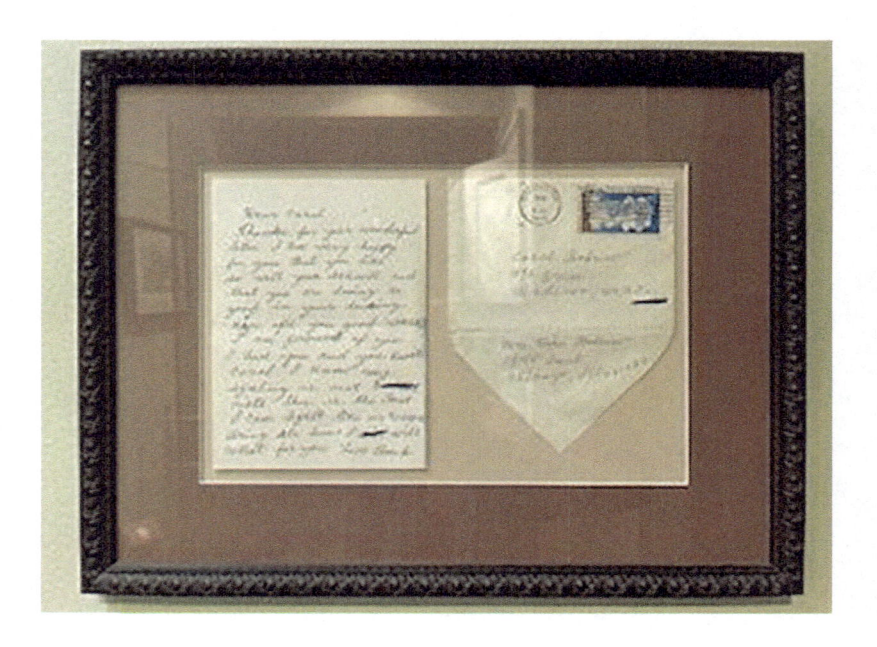

CAROL BOBROW

My grandmother's letter rests in a dark frame on a dark mat beside its white envelope which is open, the triangular flap lifted up, causing it to resemble the small white house I was living in my junior year of college when this letter arrived over fifty years ago.

The blue ink looks fresh, having been pressed hard into the page, its script a little jagged as if the words had been rambunctious and with effort were reined in—order was restored with a generous space between each word and its neighbor. Letters are of varying sizes, but sentences lie ruler-straight, and the margin is clear and even; capital letters have been given the dignity of a little flourish. This letter was not written by a hand at ease with writing, but like her tidy, immaculate apartments, there is order, care and deliberateness.

"Bauby" was a pillar of my life, the person who cherished me, the person who taught me I was lovable. We spent many weekends together in her ever-changing string of apartments, riding buses to visit relatives who came from various European countries—France, Germany, Czechoslovakia, Poland, Russia; conversations were a mix of English and Yiddish which I didn't understand but loved to listen to.

Our afternoons were spent in and out of the shops along Devon Avenue—the fruit market, the butcher, the bakery, even the Kosher ice cream store, in her never ending quest to put weight on me. At home in the green-lawned suburbs, my friends hung out at the beach or the mall, but I had no regrets for I had been transported to a world of another time and another place.

At the end of the day Bauby and I sat on the worn back steps of her building, taking in the view of Chicago rooftops at dusk, a section of the Chicago *Sun-Times* beneath us to keep our bottoms clean,

Bauby died a few years after writing my letter—the emptiness was immeasurable. I could not bear to let her go. I thought I caught glimpses of her on the "El" platform, or waiting for the cross light at Devon and Western, shopping bag in hand, babushka on her head. The sightings haunted me, then disappeared.

I understood my loss to be part of a larger tide of loss as, one by one, European Jews of her generation disappeared from the world, taking with them their humor, their warmth, and the weight they carried with them of pogroms and Czarist Russia and the rise of the Russian revolution—their history as heavy on their shoulders as the sodden woolen coats of Chicago's winters.

One day, I knew, Yiddish-crafted English would no longer be heard; a language that seemed to float on a sea of irony, where single words were capable of expressing whole ideas—so many of them funny, making our own language feel flat and unimaginative. It was a language that required amplification by animation—shrugs, hand gestures, lifted eyebrows, or a downturn of the mouth.

That world returns to me in my grandmother's letter. In her phonetic spelling I hear the richness of her voice. She tells me that she knows her "spaling is not riete," but it is the best she can do, "like in roshen." She tells me she is proud of me and that she loves me. I hear her voice, and in my mind's eye I see her give a soft pat of the air with her hand as if to signify the end of a thought put properly to rest.

This is all that I have of my grandmother, but it is enough.

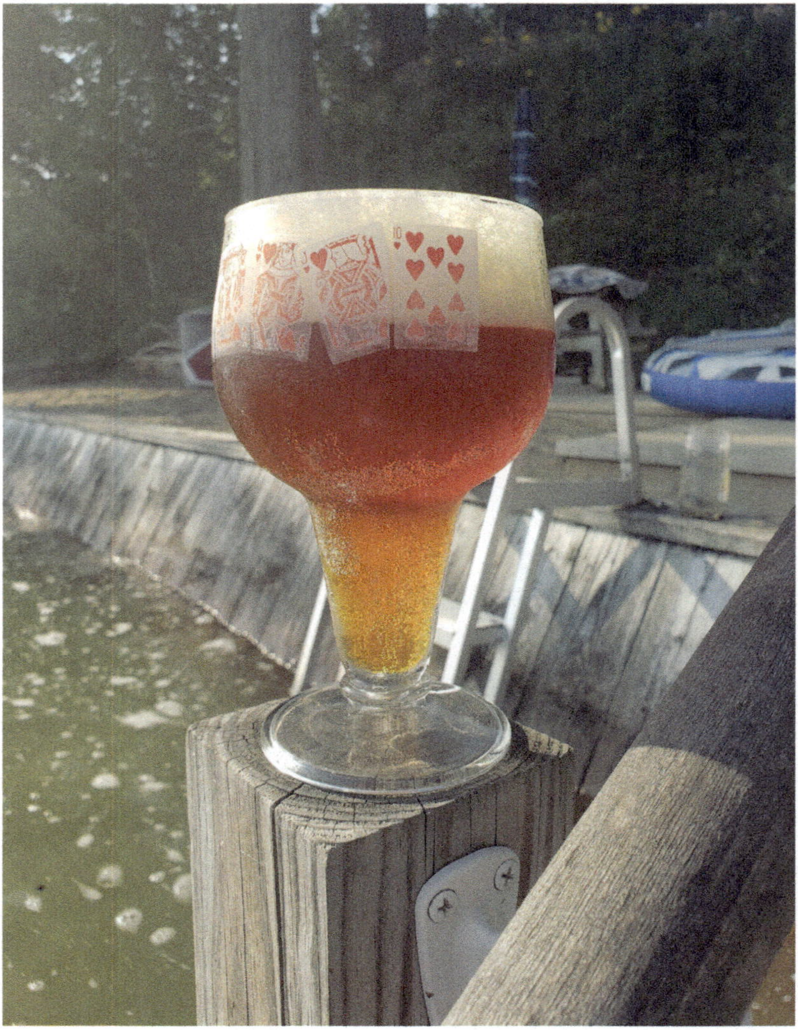

JAMES FINN GARNER

When my parents were newly married, friends in Chicago threw them a "bar shower." The gifts at that event were things like Tom Collins glasses, cocktail shakers and strainers. The one surviving gift set are beer glasses decorated with various poker hands. On this glass, one of six I still have, you can just make out that the playing cards on it are a "Royal Flush," which is also printed on the other side. (This glass is full of my homebrew beer, but that's a story for another time.) Before they were run through the dishwasher neglectfully, the blacks, whites and reds of the cards were quite vivid.

My dad was a beer drinker, and these were his go-to glasses. The golden Stroh's beer that filled it had an ethereal quality when I was little. Everything about Dad had an ethereal quality because he was a man of few words and left a lot to his sons' imaginations. I can remember sitting in his lap while he watched football games on TV, the smell of Right Guard and Vitalis, the warmth of the flesh that surrounded me like a nest. He would sing fight songs for schools that I don't think existed, and make references to Bronko Nagurski, whom I was SURE never existed. Whoever would name their kid BRONCO? He gave me sips of his beer, which I hated but loved.

These glasses give off an air of mid-1950s surety. Conviviality and confidence. Neighborhood cocktail parties, bonhomie and optimism. I grew up in the Detroit suburbs. The early 1960s was a bustling time there, witnessing a prosperity (for most) that wasn't seen again until Silicon Valley. Soon the civil rights movement and the Vietnam protests commanded people's attention, and auto executives began wearing wider lapels, though not the guys in finance, like my dad. I wonder if he ever reflected on these beer glasses, whether they ever gave him a pang of nostalgia, or a frisson of regret or loss, or an amazement at the velocity/rapacity of Time.

Neighborhood cocktail parties became fewer and fewer as families grew older and the neighbors hit later middle age. My dad was a terrible loner and didn't miss them. His habit was to go to what Michiganders call the "party store" at 10 pm to buy the next morning's *Free Press* and a quart of beer. He would then pore over that paper in his boxers and drink that Stroh's. I don't think he was an alcoholic, but the beer did help kill that taciturn, thoughtful man at an early age. And with him went his thoughts—about marriage, his sons, happiness, God and the future. When I drink from these glasses now, I toast him quietly, wishing for him a few more years of life, enjoyment and contemplation.

Storied Stuff

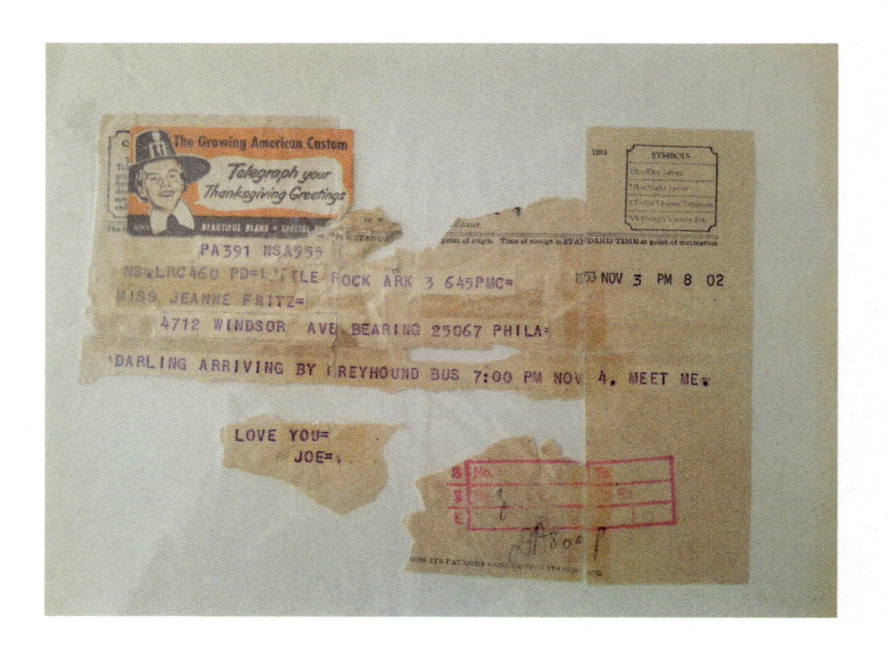

CATHY KINARD

She pulled out a telegram that she had kept that was sent by my father. The paper was fragile, and pieces of the paper were missing. It was dated November 3, 1953. She said, "I think you should have this," as she handed it to me.

I placed the pieces on the kitchen table to read the message. The memory of that day and the visceral reaction I had when reading the telegram is still fresh in my mind.

"Mom! Do you see what this says?"

She looked at me with a confused look on her face. "I don't know what you mean."

I read the entire telegram out loud to her and still she didn't understand.

My father came back into my mother's life after an absence of three years on November 4, 1953.

My father married my mother on November 24, 1953.

My father died…exactly twelve years later on November 4, 1965.

For all those years, she held that telegram never understanding the meaning of the message. My mother was a woman who did not hold on to keepsakes, and so there was a reason unknown why this treasure survived one of the routines purges she had done of the past.

She handed it to me. I put the telegram in an envelope for preservation. Eventually I put it into an album where it has remained since that day. Perhaps she knew that one day I would want to tell their story.

In those twelve years they lived a lifetime.

It wasn't an easy twelve years. It was an everyday struggle. For all the struggles that they had, I know that the foundation that kept them together was love, and their four little children.

Mom lived 45 years longer than my father did and created a new life. And it certainly was not her happily ever after.

Storied Stuff

KATHRYN L. KAPLAN

One part of our backyard in Mexico was so overgrown that only when we started hacking branches and brambles did we spot an old, discarded water tank by the fence that ended our property. Not familiar with this type of utility, we asked our landlord if he could pick it up and discard it. Always one to avoid extra work or expense, he of course said no.

Patrick, my ever-creative husband, said, "It looks like a yellow submarine—let's paint it." So we dragged the thing to an open lawn area by the house, cleaned it up, and made a plan. Using photos we found online, we sketched the Beatles' yellow submarine on one side. Then we bought yellow, red, black, and light blue paint. Day after day we worked, reveling in having time to do such a frivolous project in contrast to consulting remotely with clients in New York City.

While Patrick took the lead, he left me to paint the Fab Four looking out of the four portholes. I was so relieved when he finally said, "Perfect." Then he went back for some real work, leaving me to sketch *and* paint the Octopus's Garden on the other side. When he returned, he added a turtle, a few more fish, and hugged me, proclaiming, "Done!"

Then he got cancer and died. But before his last month, he told the gardeners to make a circular path that I could walk when it was too hard for me to walk to town. With my diminishing eyesight, I began a morning ritual with my white kitty to do meditation in motion, connecting to Patrick and walking through my grief. My first glance was always the grounded octopus (me), the two sea horses who mate for life (our undying relationship), and the happy bubbles from the flat fish, which always elevated my spirits. As I'd round the bend towards the yellow submarine, I'd look at the portholes of John, Paul, George, and Ringo and nod saying, "Perfect, perfect, perfect, perfect."

On September 11, 2024, I got the fateful text from my landlord in Spanish. "I'm sorry, but you have to move." I had two and a half months to find a new home. What a shock. He had promised I could stay forever! But there's no such thing. I'm grateful to have had seven years here, four with Patrick and three to move through grief and create a new life.

I'm getting pushed out of the nest and have to believe it is to nudge me toward the next seven-year phase. Every time I moved from DC to New York, apartment to apartment, Patrick helped me—cleaning to perfection, hanging pictures, picking out furniture, and making a house a home. This time, I'll put together a team to assist me, but it's not the same.

The only happy thought is that I found a new home for our yellow submarine. I had thought I'd be giving it to my friend Ana, who has a home in the country, but after viewing sixteen houses over four weeks, I found *the one*. It's close by and not only has room for our signature project, but also a fenced yard for my kitty. Patrick would be proud, and I'm thrilled. Full speed ahead!

Storied Stuff

JUDI GEAKE

Every time I look at the pictures of Howard and Greg shown here, I'm reminded that BOTH personalities were not always as they appeared. Greg was occasionally a sullen child. He was slow to smile and often withheld a smile altogether when there was a camera present. Howard was called "Grumpa" by all the grandchildren; he had the reputation of being a curmudgeon, a rather sullen adult.

In these photos, however, something Howard said struck him and Greg as very funny, and I just happened to have my camera ready. I don't remember what triggered these pictures. I was probably focused more on capturing the moment on film than remembering the occasion.

I do, however, remember what triggered the older pictures of my two sons. Jim was telling David a joke that contained what he thought was a swear word, "ass," and tried to keep his brother from repeating it in front of me. Again, I was fortunate to have had a camera ready and was able to capture the moment.

The pictures of Howard and Greg always recall the photos of Jim and David. After I give the pictures to Greg for his wedding, I hope he and his wife, Sydney, will hang them somewhere in their new apartment as a reminder that there was aways a happy little boy hidden under Greg's sometimes grumpy childhood face, and there was always a funny grandfather behind the often "grumpy" grandfather facade.

COURIER
Tuesday, April 22, 1969—3

'OH DAD' REHEARSAL

University of Illinois sophomore Robert Griffard, left, and junior Joe Garber run through their lines in a dress rehearsal of the New York comedy hit "Oh Dad, Poor Dad" at the Lincoln Hall Theater. The play, being staged by the University Theater, opens Wednesday night in Lincoln Hall.

JOE GARBER

It has often been said : "A picture is worth a thousand words." Today I will limit it to no more than 250.

It was early 1969. I had recently transferred to the University of Illinois in Champaign and, much to my parents' dismay, I had chosen to change my major from Architecture to Theatre.

Perhaps luck rather than talent resulted in my being cast in the university's production of "Oh Dad, Poor Dad ..." by Arthur Kopit. On my first day of rehearsal I met Robert (Bob) Griffard who had been cast in the leading role of Jonathan. Bob and I had a few short scenes together. All these years later, among items packed away in my garage, I found the press clipping shown here.

Little did I know that saving that clipping would memorialize a life-changing event. Our friendship evolved during the show, and here we are over fifty years later. I feel fortunate beyond words to still have Bob Griffard in my life as a best friend.

During the last five decades, we have shared living spaces together, traveled together, celebrated at each other's weddings, seen our children grow into young adults, laughed while together and as a foursome with our spouses. We cherish the many good times together and support each other during the difficult times. I have an everlasting friendship that simply began from being cast in a play by Arthur Kopit.

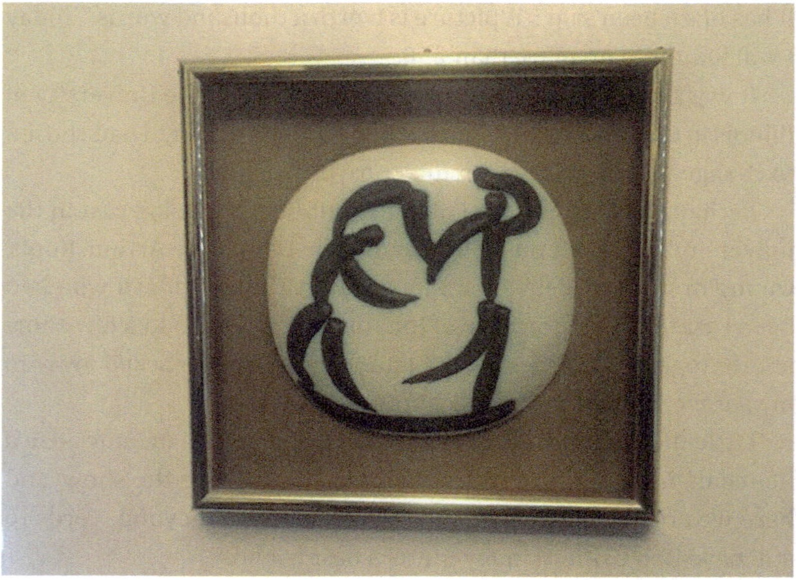

LARRY GRITTON

Jennifer and I were married in May, 1972. Of course we registered for wedding gifts at Marshall Fields, actually viewing the items at the store since there was no internet or online access. I have retained dishware, glassware and cutlery from then, but I doubt I still have anything else from the registry.

We did receive gifts from guests and friends that were not on the registry. I know we received a pewter tea service from Elaine Fiffer, but the one that stands out the most is the genuine Picasso Plate pictured here, given by friends Steve, Bill, Penny and Wendy.

This gift occupies a place of honor in my den, where I spend too much time watching TV or reading, especially during 2020, and serves as a reminder of how special family and friends can be. Our wedding was a time to celebrate with both family and friends, though sadly the family has thinned out over the years – Jennifer, my mom and dad, my in-laws Millie and Frank Levy, my *machetunim* Faye and Fred Tatel, two aunts and three uncles, and Sam Tomasello, my current wife Sara's younger brother. The Plate helps me remember them.

I am fortunate to have attended junior high at Central School in Glencoe, IL, class of 1964—in my mind the greatest single school class of all time. Sixty-plus years later we still connect, having reunions, golf outings, bar and bat mitzvahs, weddings and long weekends, and the communication is in person and not only on Facebook, although there are Growing Up Glencoe and Central Glencoe '64 groups. I have friends that are not from Glencoe, but there is something very special about the Glencoe friends. Spouses have been incorporated into the group as honorary members.

The four friends who gave me the Plate remain good friends to this day, and the Plate helps me think about them and my good fortune in having so many friends. While the Plate has increased substantially in monetary value, its value to me cannot be measured in money. It represents my life and fortunes, good and bad.

Storied Stuff

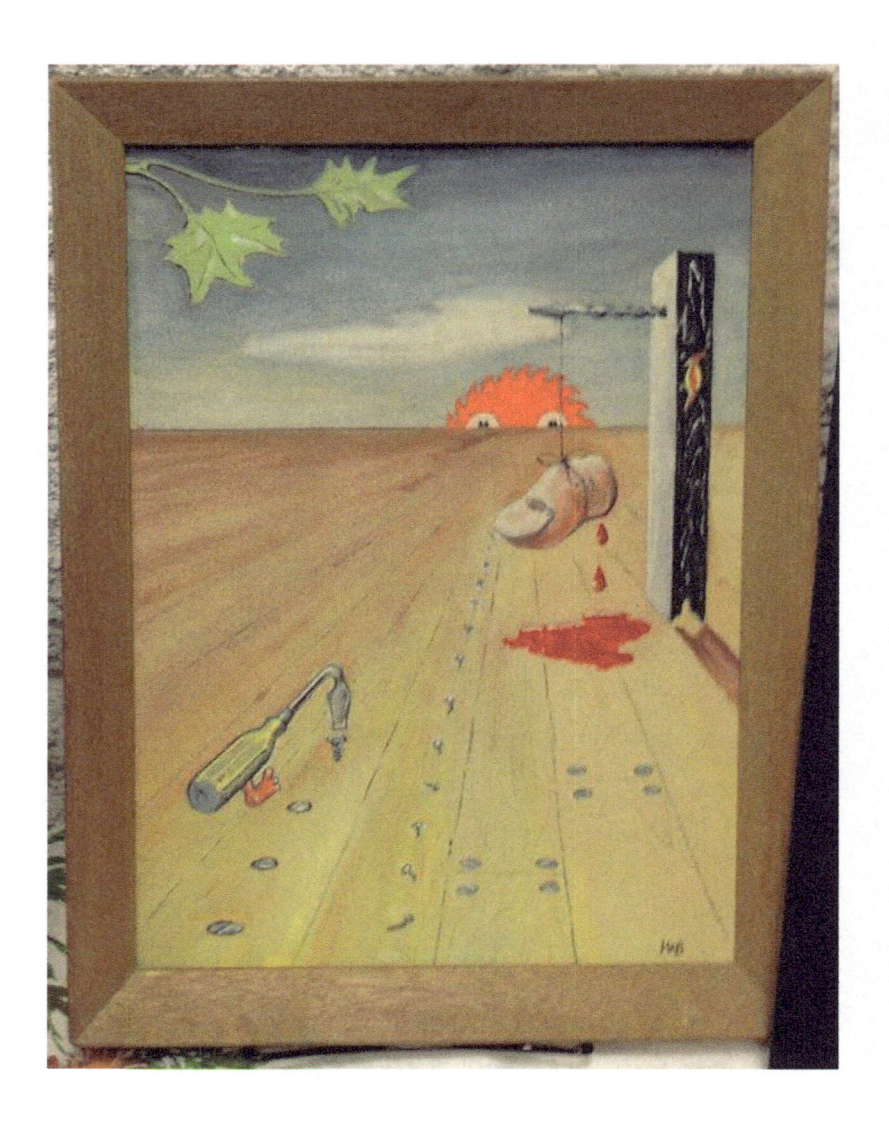

SUSIE BUTTERFIELD

Growing up in the '50s, my favorite gifts were Paint by Number sets. With the pictures came little numbered pots of paint that you used to paint the picture, according to the numbers on the picture.

There was always paint left, and those partially filled or unused pots were used by my dad to begin a long lifetime of talented drawing and painting.

Born in 1916, Dad started out as a drafting student in high school, even selling model airplane plans to magazines at age 18. Years later, after serving in WWII, getting married, having children, and making a living as a cabinet maker and carpenter, Dad renewed his interest in art.

One day, he took those leftover pots of paint and created his first oil painting: "A Woodworker's Nightmare." Did I mention he had a very good sense of humor? Eventually, he was able to buy better painting supplies and spent many hours creating his unique and precise pieces of art. He painted mostly with oils, though for about the last ten years of his life, he turned to pen and ink as his medium of choice. His favorite subjects were airplanes and trains, exact in so many details.

Today, my favorite painting of his is still "A Woodworker's Nightmare."

Storied Stuff

JULIE COWAN

As I pick out a blue pastel stick from the wooden box and apply the powdery hue to a print, I remember my parents' friend, Hermine. She was so different from my mother—tall, delicate, and soft-spoken. Hermine was an artist. I had never been around artists before and could ask her questions that were not relevant in our house. Hermine and Jack, her husband, lived in Chicago in an apartment that had original art hanging on the walls. How daring and cosmopolitan!

Hermine passed away when I was a young teenager. Jack gifted her spectacular Grumbacher Pastel set to me. Ninety colors, the fancy box, the soft protective tissue inside, the set travels with me and continues to contribute to my art practice. Hermine is with me, too.

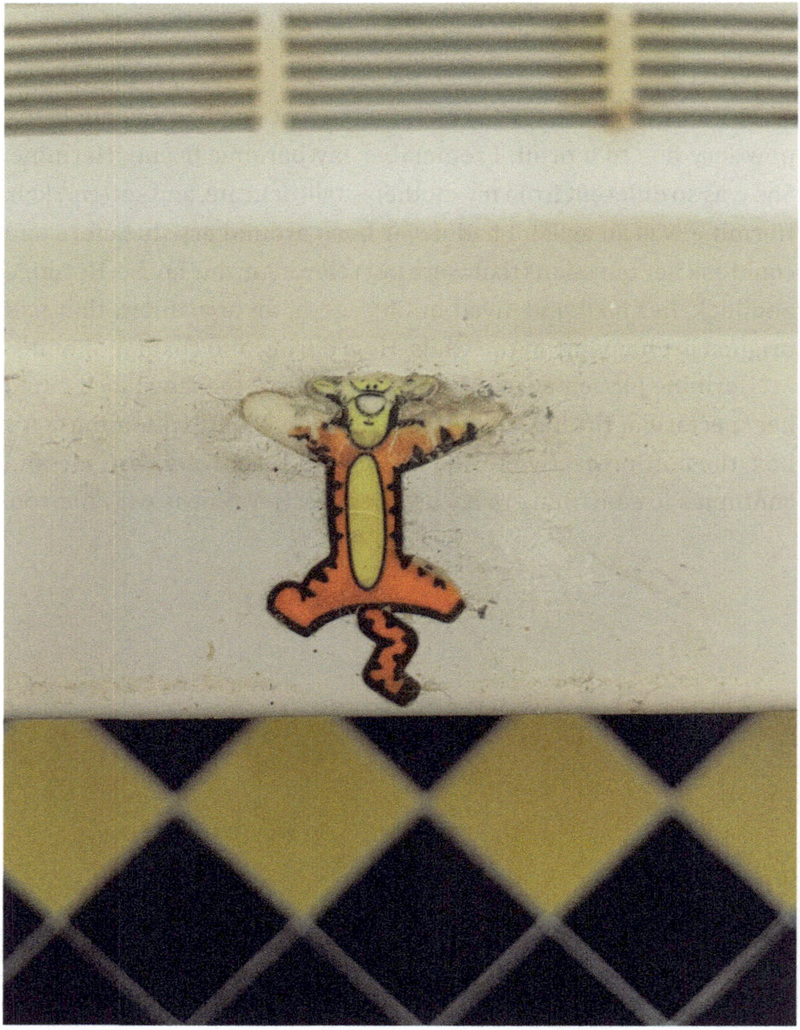

LILLIAN DAILEY

I gave my dad a sticker of the Winnie the Pooh character Tigger one Saturday morning when I was four, interrupting his pancake cooking because it felt essential to share. He stuck it on the vent hood, front and center, fresh from the sticker sheet. A layer of grime and years of cooking oils surrounding the sticker give it an ethereal glow. Years of spatter from Sunday morning bacon and boiling pasta water have immortalized him beneath a varnish of sorts.

The long existence of the Tigger sticker as a pillar of our kitchen shows the love and care that my dad puts into everything. He could have taken the sticker and thrown it away, or scraped it off after a day or two, but he has left it there for sixteen years. When cleaning the vent hood, he deliberately works around Tigger to avoid damaging him in any way. These actions mirror the care and patience that he has shown to me and my sister throughout our entire lives, from helping us make our beds, helping us through hard schoolwork, and teaching us so much of what we know.

Tigger has had a front row seat to my sister's and my childhoods, watching us turn from kids playing with dried pasta and rice on the floor into fully fledged adults, cooking dinner for the family. Tigger, with his bouncy tail and raised arms, has cheered us on from kindergarten through senior year as we ate breakfast, cried over math homework with our dad, and returned from late night swim meets in high school.

Having now left for college, I find solace in the knowledge that Tigger will be waiting for me, stuck to the vent hood, every time I come back home.

Storied Stuff

ROBERT BISSELL

I don't know when WhiskerFace first arrived at our home. Certainly before I was three. From my earliest memory, he is a constant bedtime presence - and an extraordinary story teller.

And he was not a toy - meaning I was not allowed to play with him. Rather he sat on my father's hand, telling a story. When the story was over, he left with my father. Under adult supervision, I was occasionally allowed to gently hold WhiskerFace, permitted even to wear him on my hand. But never to play with him.

The stories always involved WhiskerFace ... and me. Sometimes a friend would be missing and WhiskerFace and I would venture forth—hiking through the forest, or canoeing across the lake, or pedaling our bikes down the path. Eventually, we'd solve the mystery, of course.

Or a stuffed rabbit, one of WhiskerFace's friends, would set off on some harebrained scheme and we'd have to rescue our comrade and set things right. Often the stories were all adventure and fun. But sometimes they carried a moral: Be Kind. Be Helpful. Be Respectful. And Have Fun! WhiskerFace, you see, could also be quite silly.

The stories worked: I usually did not attempt to delay bedtime. And I bet they continued until I was 9 or 10. Even when I was older, WhiskerFace would make unexpected appearances on the hand of my father.

When I had children, WhiskerFace moved to my home and continued his stories. I maintained the same rules: Gentle holding was fine - but no rough play! After all, he was in his thirties then.

WhiskerFace must be in his seventies now. But, unlike the rest of us, he hasn't aged a whisker. And now he is entertaining the fourth generation of our family. My granddaughters love WhiskerFace - and love his storied adventures, which, of course, always involve them. They are respectful and kind to him. And WhiskerFace always makes them the heroines of each bedtime story.

    I guess it's obvious that WhiskerFace has accomplished one more feat within our family: He has connected the four generations. My father never knew his great-granddaughters, but his effect on them is quite real.

Storied Stuff

BARBARA WALTER HETLER

Christmas 1967. A long-eared, 28" tall, bright orange plush dog was presented as a promotion by the *Chicago Tribune*. If you ordered a subscription, you'd receive the Cuddly Dudley dog.

Our son John was 9 months old, so we thought Cuddly would make a great Christmas gift. Oh the pictures we would have in our son's "Precious Baby Book" of him hugging his new stuffed toy.

For years the life-sized Cuddly Dudley sat in a corner of John's room. His ears and nose had cookie stains from being loved. The ribbon around his neck was frayed, but his perfect long red tongue still hung at a rakish angle from his mouth.

Cuddly remained in John's room until we decided to re-do the bedrooms. All stuffed animals were given away, save Cuddly, who was relocated to the basement. *Temporarily*, we said.

Fast-forward several decades. Our church was having a rummage sale. After filling several boxes, I noticed Cuddly Dudley. *Might as well take him, too.* The trunk was already filled. I set him carefully on the passenger seat, securing him with the belt.

On the ride to the church, I kept staring at Cuddly sitting beside me looking a bit shaggy, but as adorable as the day he had come to our house.

We pulled into the church parking lot. I unloaded the trunk. Then I started to lift Cuddly Dudley. Those bright eyes, that red tongue. I just couldn't do it.

Cuddly no longer is by himself in the basement. He's been dusted off, has a new ribbon 'round his neck and sits proudly in a bedroom we reserve for our grandchildren when they come to visit. And sitting on a bookshelf in the same room is the "Precious Baby Book" with the photo of John hugging Cuddly Dudley.

Storied Stuff

JENNY KLEIN

A push puppet is a simple wooden toy where one presses the thumb on the bottom to make the puppet dance, wag a tail, shake a head, bend a knee or collapse altogether. I own this classic spotted dog push puppet, which is certainly vintage by now considering how long I've had it. I laughed when I went online to research the common name for the toy and found a YouTube video on how to play with it.

The toy spent several years in a box tagged "Jenny's things" in the basements of my parents' homes and mine until about ten years ago when I dug it out and remembered the simple joy it rendered.

On weekends, when I was a little girl I'd wake up early and play with the toys in my bedroom. The house was silent and so was I. Like any little kid, I enjoyed a good secret. Those mornings were hush hush. While everyone slept, a busy, imaginary world with nary a murmur unfolded in my room. One vignette for the spotted dog involved lying in bed and pulling my pink, blue, and yellow striped blanket over my bent upright knees to create a mountain. The spotted dog climbed the mountain, wagged his tail and hopped back down only to collapse. He hiked a lot of miles in the early 1960s.

Today, the spotted dog has the run of the house sitting on the dining room table, my desk or the kitchen window ledge. Age hasn't affected his flexibility. He still tilts his head, wiggles his tail and makes me smile.

Storied Stuff

DENNIS BARON

I was born and grew up in a train town. The Illinois Central Railroad is the reason for the existence of Kankakee, Illinois. Throughout my life, trains, some rumbling and some gliding—including the City of New Orleans—made their way through the center of town. They were an essential feature of the city's life, and part of this was the ever-present, but unpredictable, train whistle.

Like many children growing up in the Fifties and early Sixties, I had a train set, complete with a nicely detailed blue Chesapeake & Ohio engine. It was wonderful. The engine had a whistle, under the control of the operator, but it could not compare to the train whistle of the real thing that was the chorus of the daily soundtrack of the city. The sound of the train whistle was at the same time both haunting and sorrowful and exhilarating and promising.

As a little kid, falling asleep, listening to the train whistle, I thought of the faraway and exotic places where the train was heading and pictured my future life in these places. Well, although the train famously pulled out of Kankakee, I didn't. After going away for college and law school, I chose to return to work and raise a family.

At all times, the train whistle has continued to hold me in its spell. I rate my days by the number of times I consciously hear that sound, treating it as a Muslim might react to the call to prayer, or a Catholic responding to the Angelus. It assembles my focus.

Happily, the tradition lives on. I have the fabulous good fortune to live three blocks from my son, his wife, and their little boy, who, likewise, live well within the allure of the train.

Not long after he was a year old, he started making a downward gesture like the pulling of a cord, with a sparkle in his eye, whenever the train whistle floated over our neighborhood.

Storied Stuff

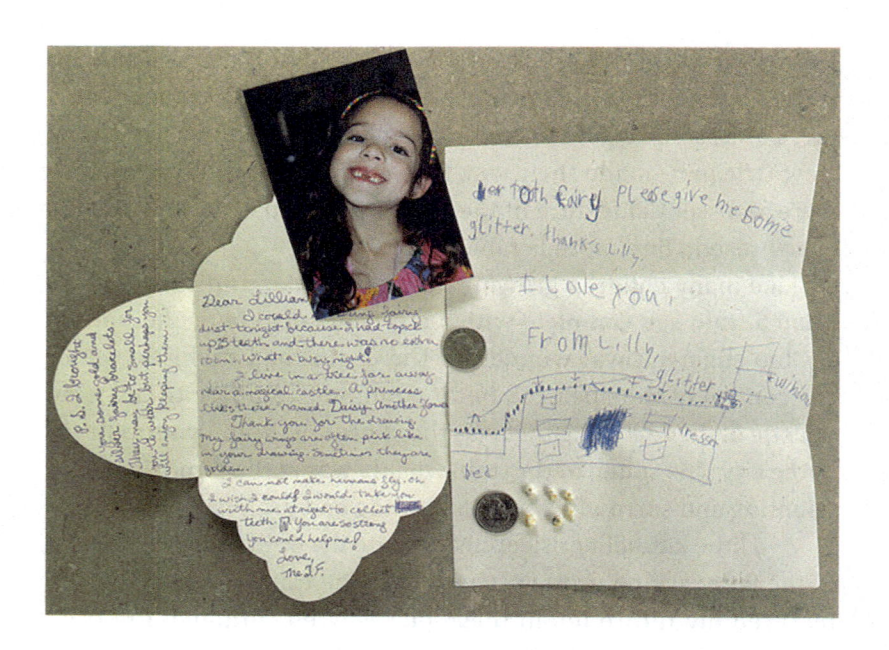

LISA HART

When my daughter Lilly was a young girl, she had a love affair with the tooth fairy. She was obsessed with communicating with the fairy and would leave elaborate drawings and messages for the fairy every time she lost a tooth. She once orchestrated a meeting of the Tooth Fairy and the Easter Bunny by saving her tooth until Easter eve and then leaving her tooth and instructions for the tooth fairy to go to the living room and talk with the Easter Bunny.

Of course, I was the tooth fairy and I loved the fantasy and play as much as she did. The fairy left a trail of fairy dust (glitter) along the window sill and across the dresser leading to under Lilly's pillow. Lilly's letters included many questions about what it is like to live in the fairy world. The fairy always left either a letter, a small gift, or a drawing along with a shiny Susan B. Anthony dollar.

We have a box in the closet with all of the letters, teeth and small gifts from that time. It's like a time capsule of Lilly's imaginative childhood.

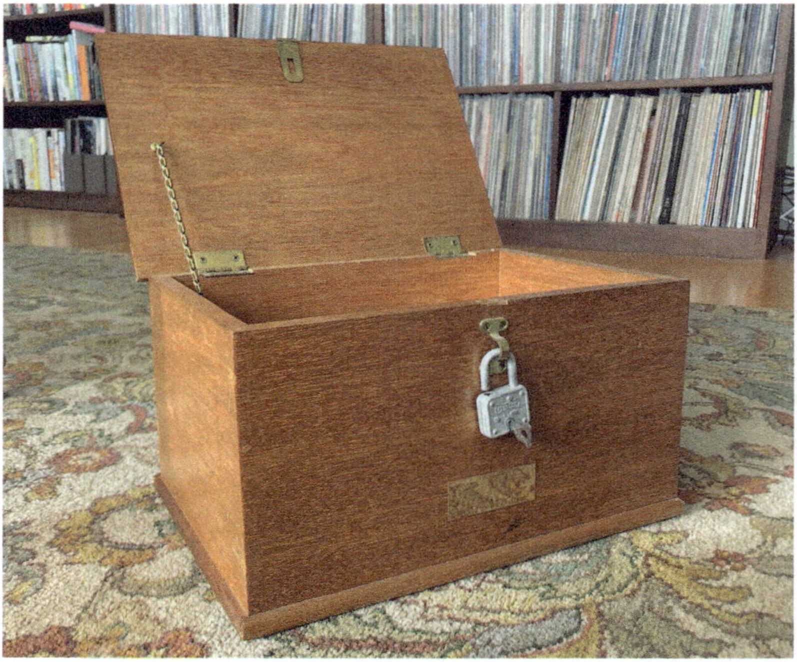

KEIR GRAFF

When I was probably seven years old, my maternal grandfather gave me a wooden treasure chest he'd made himself. His style was functional, not ornate, but to me the chest was the most beautiful thing in the world. It had hinges, a chain to keep the lid from flopping backward, a hasp and padlock—and a brass plate with my initials.

The chest was treasure in itself, but I filled it with more: coins, polished rocks, a homemade porcupine-quill necklace, a silver-and-turquoise ring I bought on a family road trip to the Southwest, bullet shells I picked up in the alley. A cedar box from a Yellowstone Park gift shop, a chest within the chest, protected the most valuable items.

I kept the box locked and carefully hidden, hoarding my wealth, greeting the world with confidence born from the knowledge of my secret fortune.

This year, in lockdown, I weeded the contents, tossed some, gave some to my kids, and sent some to the Salvation Army. I couldn't decide how to get rid of the box itself—after all, it had my initials on it.

I kept it. I wish I'd kept every piece of treasure, too. But I'm finding new things to put into it. Silver dollars from my paternal grandfather. Small military artifacts from my historian uncle. The keys to the Mustang I sold when I moved to Chicago.

Everyone should have a treasure chest.

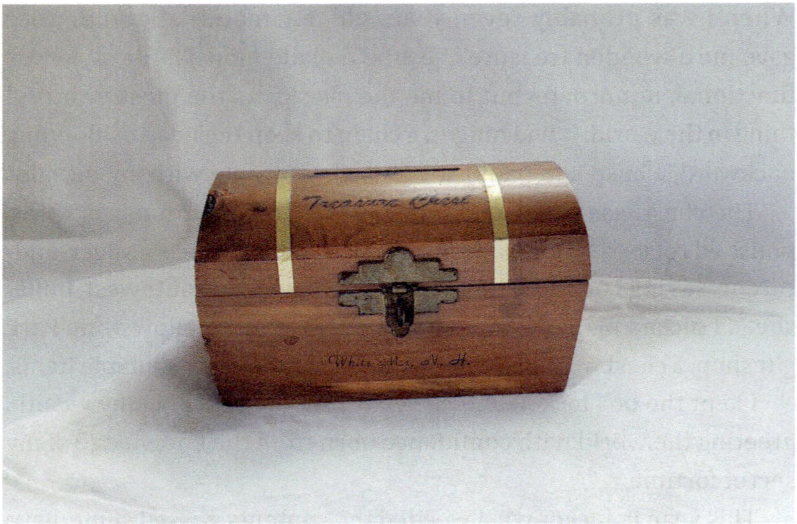

MARYLOU DiPIETRO

When I was five my parents took us on a trip to the White Mountains. I had only seen pictures of mountains, so the idea of seeing real mountains filled me with excitement.

The two things I remember about that day were my father lifting me up to look into what looked like a gigantic parking meter to see the Old Man in the Mountain and going to a place called The Flume. I had a feeling in the pit of my stomach that I had never felt before as we zig-zagged into a magical place which I secretly believed was the center of the earth.

My memory of coming out of The Flume is not as clear as the sadness I felt that the day was coming to an end. As if my parents knew how we felt, they announced that we could each pick one souvenir from the shop that was built into the side of the mountain.

While my sisters and brother examined each of the souvenirs on shelves they could reach, I knew immediately which souvenir I wanted. It was a child-size treasure chest with a lock and key and the words "White Mountains, N.H." written on it. When I opened the lid, the smell of my mother's cedar chest escaped into the air. I remember holding my treasure chest on my lap all the way home, not knowing it would be the memory of that day that I would keep locked inside forever.

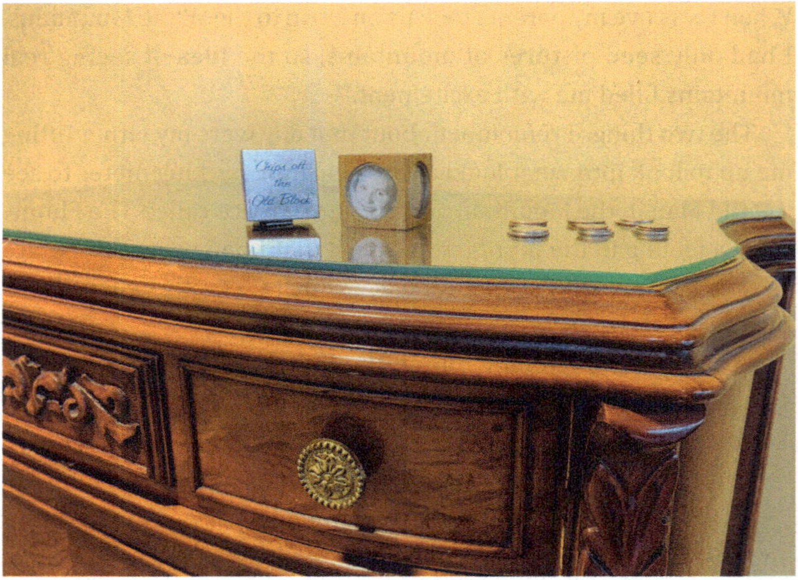
Chips off the Old Block

GEORGE KOVAC

My father was a precise and orderly man. The top of his dresser, a solid highboy, held only three things: the keys to the family Buick, six stacks of coins, and a pair of wooden cubes. Dad set the coins out early Sunday morning, one stack for each child to deposit in the collection basket at Sunday mass.

The tops of the wooden cubes bore the inscription "Chips off the Old Block." Each side had a recess for a photo, and so my father inserted a picture of each of his children. My mother and paternal grandmother filled the remaining spaces. Every day my father would rotate the blocks ninety degrees, so that a new pair of children or mothers would face forward. I worked out the math. I would be featured twice a week for three weeks, then only one day the next week. Repeat. Always paired with the same sister.

My dad never updated the photos, the family was frozen in time. I was always a second grader, smiling above my bowtie in my school picture. By the time I was an adolescent, I grew to resent those photos. I was growing up, but my father still saw me as a little boy.

After my parents died, to my surprise, I kept the wooden cubes.

My oldest sister turned 80 in April. Because of the pandemic, the celebration was held on Zoom. On our computer screens, my brothers and sisters reassembled, images of each of us occupying our respective squares, side by side, chips off the old block.

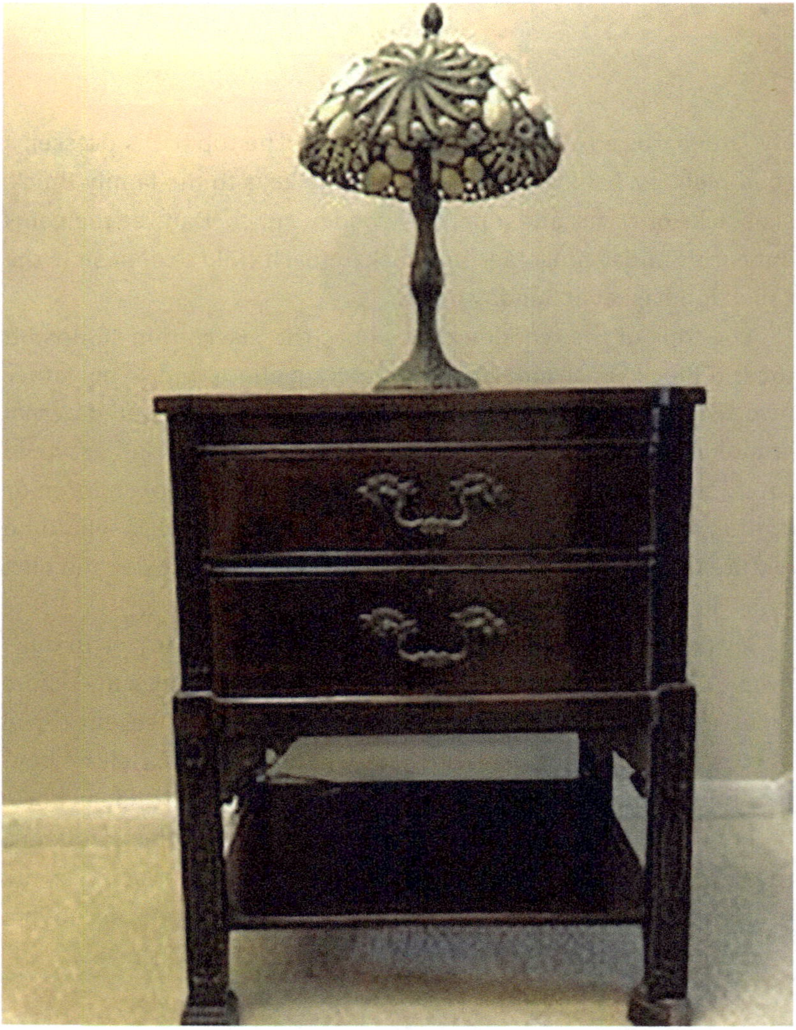

MARILYN KOCHMAN

When my mother died, the only object I wanted from her assisted living apartment was a small, mahogany nightstand. Before that, for over half a century, it stood guard on my father's side of the bed in my parents' Northeast Philadelphia, ranch-style home.

I did not hesitate for a moment when my siblings asked if I'd be interested in becoming the next owner. After hauling the nightstand 40 miles to my apartment, I placed the small piece of furniture - - and the shell-studded lamp that she loved - - in the entranceway. Now, whenever I walk into my home, I'm awash with bittersweet feelings.

As a child, I'd often wander into my parents' bedroom, sit at the edge of the bed, and stare at the nightstand's two drawers, wondering what secrets they stored. Slowly, stealthily, I'd pull open the top drawer. It was always a mess with clutter: a yellowing address book, a crinkled black-and-white Polaroid photo, a half-eaten package of mint Life Savers.

Like my parents, I have a penchant for clutter, and whenever I don't know where to store something, into one of the drawers it goes: a show schedule from the 1990 Telluride Film Festival; a Lifetime Pass to the National Parks; and a faded, red-orange wallet I once gave my mother and don't have the heart to give away.

My little mahogany nightstand is, however, so much more than a repository for random items. Today, whenever I pull open one of the drawers, I hear a familiar and heart-warming sound. It is the sound of wood scraping wood, the sound of my parents, the sound of lives that are no longer.

Storied Stuff

CHUCK FRANK

When my mom passed away 17 years ago, my siblings and I and took turns choosing items of sentimental value in her apartment. There was a large ceramic figure of a mounted St. George that ruled over the living room; a clock ringed with 12 framed avian images; a pair of black wooden shoes with marble inlays, which my wife Debbie and I claimed.

That left 50 bags for Goodwill and the contents of her desk drawers: Scratch paper, pens that skipped, paper clips, an old stapler and a plastic box filled with rubber bands.

As an afterthought, I took the box with rubber bands. Those always seem to come in handy.

The wooden shoes rest quietly in a closet now, still eye-catching but with nowhere to go. I see them every once in a while when I'm looking for something I've misplaced.

On the other hand, the box of rubber bands, with its tattered label in my mom's handwriting, is a desktop companion. I'm in and out of it regularly, depositing new rubber bands or looking for a good fit for a loose cord or a deck of cards. I think about my mom – and sometimes even have ethereal conversations with her – every time I open that box. It acts as a catalyst, and in a strange but comforting way, those rubber loops keep us connected.

Storied Stuff

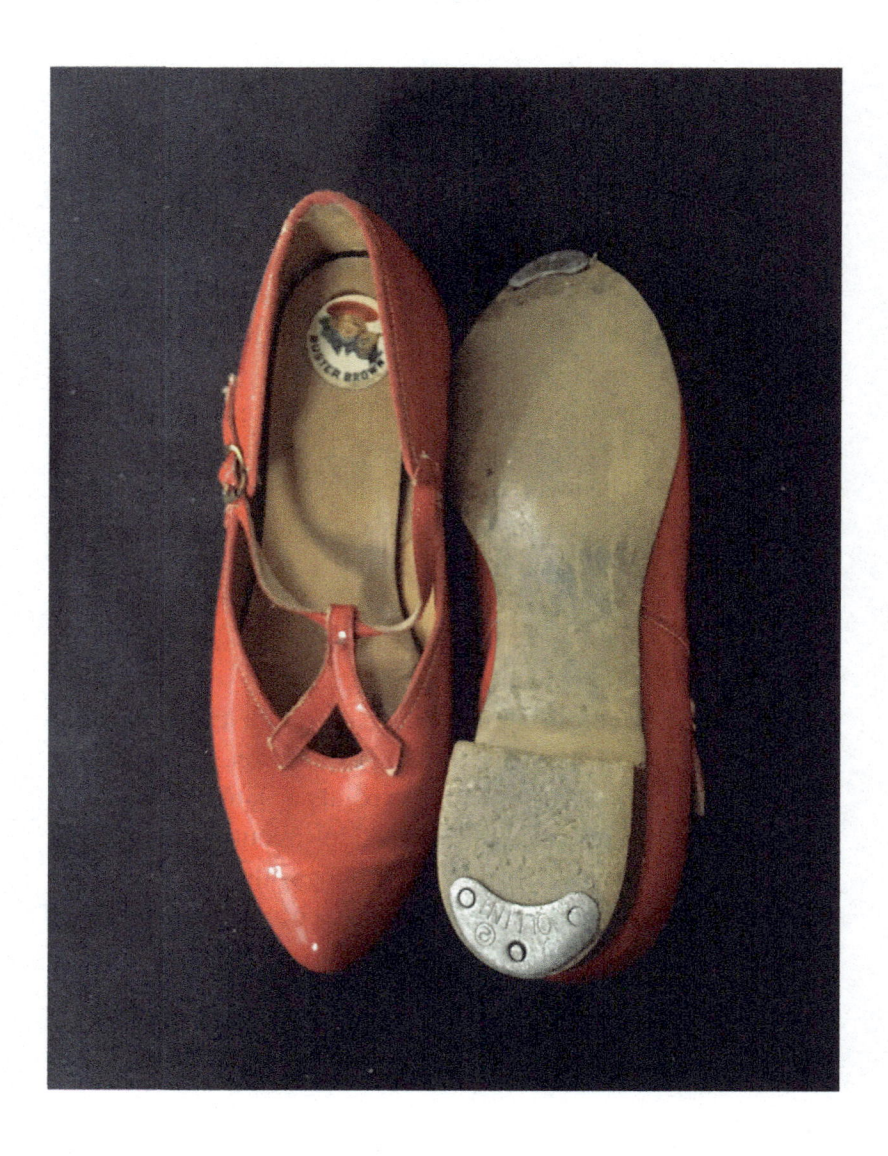

PATRICIA ADELSTEIN

When I was nine, I won the lead in the local high school play, entitled, *The Bad Seed*. In the play, my character, Rhoda, is revealed to be a psychopath. Dire events happen as a result, including a shocker ending.

I wore these red shoes throughout the play. The shoes had metal taps on the tops and bottoms of their soles. It is presumed that Rhoda killed a little boy by hitting him with her tap-laden shoes and pushing him off a dock.

I give credit to my mom for helping me learn my 200+ lines despite my reluctance to sit still. She would trap me while I was taking a bath each night. It felt so strange saying some of the lines in front of my mother! I occasionally worried that I, too, was a psychopath! But I was old enough to draw the distinction between reality and fantasy. I loved being on stage and had no problem saying these terrible lines to everyone but my mother.

When the play concluded, I flew down the main aisle of the theater to my family, screaming, "I'm glad it's over!" But I wasn't glad. Later as a teenager, in that same high school, I got on stage as often as I could.

I did not become an actor, of course. When I look at these shoes now, I think less about my lines and Rhoda and more about how I learned some lifelong lessons on that stage. I still think, at 65, I learned more on that stage than in any of my high school classes.

I learned to look people in the eye when you want them to pay attention to you. I learned how to become comfortable in my own skin when I didn't feel comfortable in my own skin. I learned that exposing yourself honestly, even though in the guise of a role, is power and real intimacy. And I learned that they eventually take away the playbook from you, so you better hurry up, do your homework, and memorize your lines!

Storied Stuff

CHUCK BROWN

"Your momma wears combat boots!"

What did that even mean? Why is that a bad thing? I'll Google it later.

Anyway, this is about my combat boots, but not my momma.

I was in the Air Force from 1996 to 2000. My service tenure is not a point of pride. It was utilitarian – i.e., I was getting people off my back because I'd flunked out of college. It also was a quiet, boring military stint, which is something a lot of kids who signed up just a year or two after me cannot say.

I became an airplane mechanic because the dad of this girl I dated had been an Air Force mechanic when he was young, and I thought he was kind of cool.

For four nondescript years, I was the worst mechanic in U.S. Air Force history. Fortunately, I knew I was bad, so I just did exactly what my supervisor (who was the best mechanic in the Air Force) told me to do. Ultimately, only one of the planes I worked on crashed and there was, thankfully, no proof that it was my fault. It collided with a German cargo plane and fell deep into the Atlantic Ocean off the west coast of Africa.

About the boots. They are steel-toed, they still fit, and they live in my garage. Somewhere between two and ten times a year, I lace them up to go blow the snow off my driveway. When I dig them out, I marvel at how long it has been and how I still feel 18 – even though I have a kid that age now. And then at some point it hits me just how lucky I was to have "fixed" planes at such a quiet, boring time.

Storied Stuff

NAN DOYAL

When my great-grandmother died, she left to me a plastic pill bottle stuffed with an old tissue. Buried in the folds of the disintegrating white pulp was a brooch and a note saying it was her most treasured possession. It was made from a pair of sterling silver eagle wings that flanked the letters R-A-F. They were fastened to a laurel wreath beneath a red enameled and diamond crown. The pin was a replica of the pilot wings that had been awarded to my grandfather, her son, when he became a Flight Lieutenant in the Royal Air Force.

My grandfather flew Bristol Blenheims. When he was twenty-three, he was shot down and killed while bombing Nazi munitions factories and shipyards in occupied Holland. He was survived by his wife and an eight-month-old son, my father.

For years my great-grandmother's brooch lay forgotten in its plastic cocoon, buried at the back of my jewelry box. I had no use for an old-fashioned pin that belonged to a woman I barely knew, given to her by a grandfather I had never met. But something made me hold on to it, if for nothing more than respect for a mother's last link to her son.

The year my own grandmother died, something inspired me to retrieve the silver pin from its hiding place. As I turned the piece between my fingers, I thought not about the man who had gifted it, but of his mother and his wife, and what *they* had given.

Military service skipped two generations in my family after WW2, and during those years some of us moved away from the country my grandfather fought for. But last November, three days before Veterans Day, my American son signed on to serve in the US Air Force as a

101

combat search and rescue operator. I could not decide whether it was irony or fate that he joined a branch of Special Operations created explicitly to rescue downed fighter and bomber pilots.

On the morning he left, I went into my jewelry box, and for the first time, I pinned that winged brooch to my chest.

Storied Stuff

MANNY BROWN

Berson, Manny M.19th: 04/05/45 Pfc36692231 Died of Wound

A young man, just out of his teens, with his whole life in front of him. A wonderful person. Known to be friendly and warm with a keen intelligence. He is called to action to defend the country he loves after Pearl Harbor is bombed by the Japanese. He is sent to the Pacific Theatre of the war, where he is wounded in combat and passes from this world in April of 1945.

A little more than ten years later, I showed up and was given the name "Manny" in honor of my Uncle Manny. I never knew him, but heard all the stories about how great a son, brother, and friend he was from my family. At an early age I could not grasp the sacrifice he made. But when I became a man at the age of thirteen, I was given this flag. His burial flag. That's when it all made sense to me.

In the late '60s and early '70s, as the Vietnam War filled every young man's world, this flag meant so much more to me. I was not a fan of the war, but if drafted and called, I would have served my country. I'm not sure why I felt strongly about this. I just felt it was the right thing to do.

Storied Stuff

NANCY HEPNER GOODMAN

"If you see a Russian flag in front of the grade school run home as fast as you can." My mother told me this during the 1962 Cuban missile crisis. I was seven years old. Mom also came up with a family code we were to use if war broke out, separating us from each other.

"*Deep in the forest lived a lively family of animals.*"

It was the first line of my favorite bedtime story, and the code would help us find each other. I didn't understand how it would work or why we needed it. It seemed like a different version of treasure hunt, a game we played for hours in the backyard. I couldn't fathom war, being separated from my parents, or having strangers raise me.

Yet in Ukraine, children are being taken to Russia and placed in new homes, with new Russian parents. Mom's fears weren't far-fetched.

War didn't break out in the United States. I quit looking for the American flag at school, and took democracy for granted. My mother never spoke about codes again, and by the 1970s she'd moved on from Russian worries to making Russian tea. This wasn't the black tea consumed by upper-class Russians in the late nineteenth and early twentieth centuries. It was a combination of Tang, ice tea concentrate, lemonade mix, sugar, cinnamon and ground cloves. She heard about it from a church friend, and joined the craze, passing it out in mason jars during the holidays.

As an Irish American, my mother loved having a cup of tea in the afternoon. She drank tea with my grandmother and then eventually she drank Russian tea with me. We'd watch the teapot until it boiled, lifting it from the burner before the high-pitched whistle. Two tablespoons of the dirt-colored concoction were measured into brown ceramic mugs, then the hot water was added. For a touch of fancy, my mother put a long stick of cinnamon into each drink. We'd sit clutching the steaming mugs in our hands, enjoying idle chatter.

I lost the handwritten Russian Tea recipe my mother gave me with her easy flow of cursive writing, so different than the jagged scribbles later in her life. The internet and store provided all the information and ingredients I needed. I mixed the tea and sipped the spicy sweetness, so soothing on bitter cold days.

I now wonder what stories parents in Ukraine whisper to their children, their own family codes, as the war rages on into a second year.

Storied Stuff

MARY LORETTA KELLY

Twenty years ago I meandered through an art fair in Woodbury, Connecticut, and picked up one of my favorite pieces of folk art. I was struck by the beauty of the design, but when I learned from the collector that it is *Petrykivka*, reverse painting-on-glass, unique to Ukraine, and the artist must paint using a mirror looking over his shoulder to see what he is doing, I had to have it. Since I can't paint in forward motion and this rendering is in reverse, I was even more enthralled and impressed.

I had no idea what the symbols meant, but with a bit of research I found that what we are witnessing from the people of Ukraine during these past weeks of horror is etched in their identity and their art. Some of the following symbols in my small (4" x 6") piece of painted glass include: the wild boar indicating incredible strength, resolute courage and fearless aggression; the third eye, which is often described as the window to the soul, but also spiritual illumination; the triangle, which represents the Trinity in its religious connotation, but also the natural elements of water, fire, air; and the firebird denoting the magical everlasting light.

This is Ukraine.

Storied Stuff

N. G. HAIDUCK

Inheritance

He wants the mortar and pestle of brass

carried by his great-grandmother from Russia

to America. Her heavy heirloom,

  not new even then, his only heirloom,

made to last: solid, dull, pitted brass,

engraved with the maker's mark in Russian.

  Never will he rub the smudge of Russia

from the pocked surface of his sole heirloom.

He strikes the pestle against mortar of brass,

ringing anew his brass heirloom from Russia.

Back story: My father-in-law, Abe, knew Neal, my husband, wanted the mortar and pestle, carried to the USA by Great-Grandma Leah, and stored by Aunt Sarah in the back of her kitchen cabinet. When Aunt Sarah died, Neal was afraid his cousin would take the mortar and pestle, and not let him have it—just because he wanted it. (She was like that.) So his father, at age 95, snuck into his sister's empty apartment and took the mortar and pestle for Neal. It's the only thing we have of our dear aunt. Our cousin never missed it.
    Abe was proud of his deed.

Storied Stuff

PEGGY HEITMANN

Great Grandmother Nina owned a teapot from China that served us hot tea and a bond that strengthened with each cup she served.

By the time she gave it to me, the bone China with pink roses brandished a chipped lip. Grandma Nina did not supply a lid when she gifted it to me, but I don't care. The pot holds grace and elegance just like the woman of my memories who lived until my sophomore year of college. All those recollections steep into a sweet jasmine flavor now that she is gone.

I do not remember the day she gave it to me. I know the rose tea pot belonged to her, but I have owned it so many years I feel like it has been in my possession all my life.

When I say that I have owned it, that part is true. The other truth hinges on how I lost my treasure. It got swooped up by a man who left me in a state of grief and anger that I caused. My teapot became a war treasure he locked away in his storage unit in New Orleans.

After the battles between my long-term partner and I cooled, we resumed our friendship. After fourteen years of separation from my cherished grandmother's teapot, he mailed it back to me. Now, I adore it as though a dear, dear companion missing in action, left on the battlefield for more than a decade finally returned home.

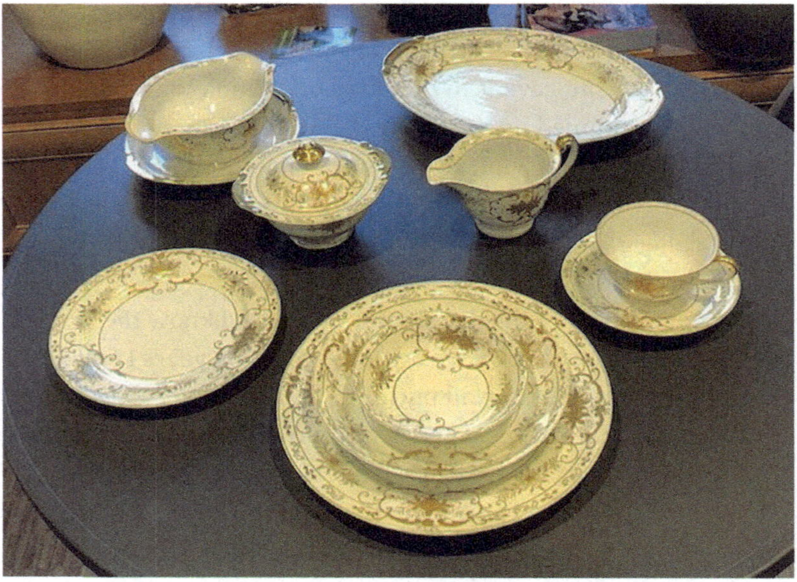

CANDICE GLICKEN

When Mom inherited her grandmother's special set of china, there were only eleven place settings. Since sets of dishware usually come in even numbers—it is, after all, a couple's world—this was a puzzle.

The story goes that our beloved Bawba was having one of her incredible family dinners and was, of course, using her fine china. Bawba kept Kosher. Kosher is a complicated dietary system used by the more religious Jewish people. The main rule is that you NEVER mix meat and dairy foods at a meal. Bawba's china had to be for meat, as brisket is a mainstay of Jewish holiday main courses. Apparently, the woman serving the food and helping clean up, put something that was used for dairy dishes in one of Bawba's bowls or plates. Catastrophe!

Bawba went to the rabbi to ask if she'd have to destroy her set of china. The rabbi listened intently to my great grandmother's tale of woe. He then told Bawba that she should bury one place setting in the backyard. The symbolic destruction of the place setting would be enough to save the rest of her precious china. So, somewhere in the backyard of a building near Kimball and Spaulding in Chicago is the twelfth place setting of Bawba's china.

I am now the proud owner of the dishes since Mom passed away and have used them on a few special occasions. I'd love to have all twelve place settings of Bawba's hand-painted, antique china. So, if you find a plate, a bowl, a cup and saucer buried in the backyard of your condo, please give me a call.

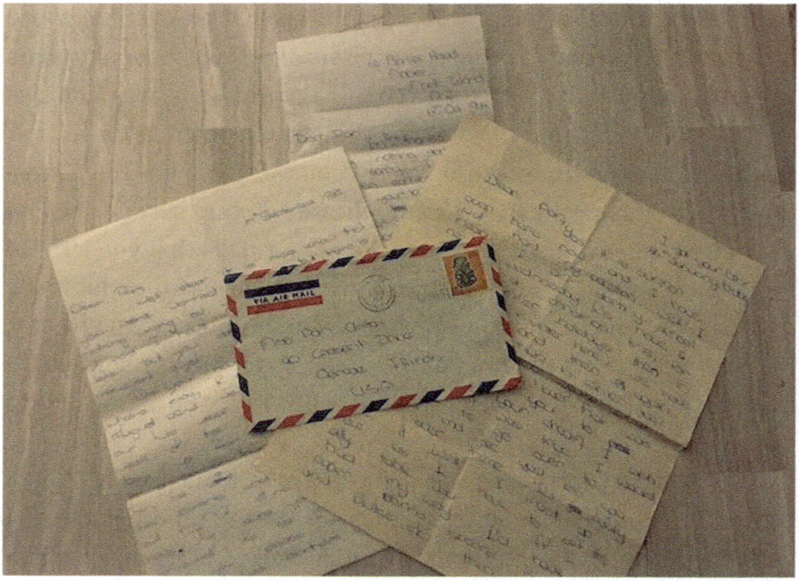
VIA AIR MAIL

PAM GASSEL

In the '60s, it was common for people to have pen pals. I was no exception. My favorite was Maureen from New Zealand. We wrote letters for two years (ages 10-12). We stopped writing for some reason, and I stashed some of her letters in a scrapbook.

Fast forward to the pandemic. One of my projects was rummaging through all I'd saved and figuring out what to do with everything. Lo and behold, I found the letters and started reading them to my family. The next thing I knew, one of my daughters was searching for Maureen on Facebook and found what looked like a match. She contacted her through Messenger, asking if she'd had a pen pal from Illinois. Within an hour, Maureen messaged her back and confirmed it! She also said, "I recently was thinking of your mother and would love to hear from her!"

Just like that, we became Facebook friends, catching up on our lives and even having our first phone conversation!

I can't believe how fast this happened. It's wild — It used to take two weeks to receive a letter and that was our only form of communication. Now, 56 years later, I saw how the power of instant technology changed the concept of pen pals, as it only took about a minute to find someone halfway around the world. It's definitely been so cool to experience renewing a friendship with someone I was close to years ago, but never met in person!

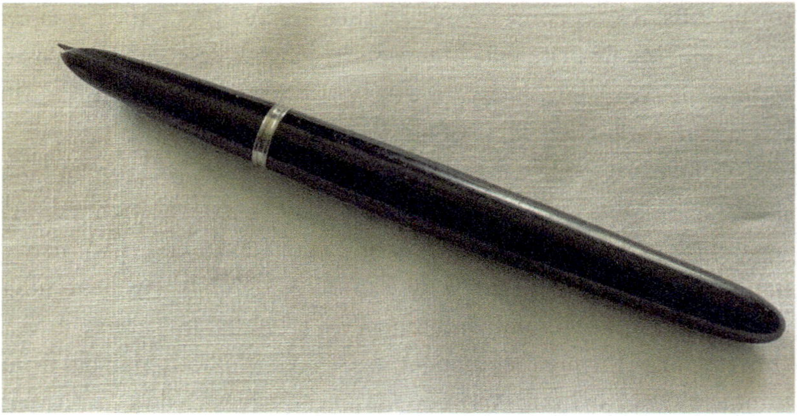

ELAINE JOHNSON

Picking through a bottomless shoebox of pencils, ballpoints and other office clutter from my parents' home, I found the keepsake that matters most to me as a writer. My mother's Parker 51 fountain pen.

The pen is a classic, but not rare. With the help of the internet, I learned the Parker 51 was one of the best-selling pens of its era. My mother's pen is from the late '40s or early '50s—the years after she left high school and before she married my dad.

Uncapped, it looks like a slim black cigar with a small nib protruding from one end. The nib is a little off-center—not by design, but due perhaps to the mechanics of my mother's handwriting over long years of use.

I remember her using that pen throughout my childhood, especially during our shopping trips to the department stores in downtown Rockford. As I stood at her elbow at the checkout counter, she would remove the silver cap with its arrow clip and pause over a sales receipt just long enough to make a series of ovals in the air. It was a Palmer penmanship exercise she learned in school. And until Parkinson's Disease erased her perfectly slanted handwriting, she always warmed up that way before putting pen to paper.

I would watch as she signed her name to the charge slip—Mrs. Raymond Johnson. That confused and annoyed me. "Your name isn't Raymond," I said, foreshadowing the cultural changes soon to come.

Eventually, the Parker 51 was sidelined by ballpoints and felt-tips, and I never asked my mother how she came to own it. Maybe she bought it as a 20-year-old bookkeeper, just starting out in the world. And if that pen could write its own story, I would know for sure.

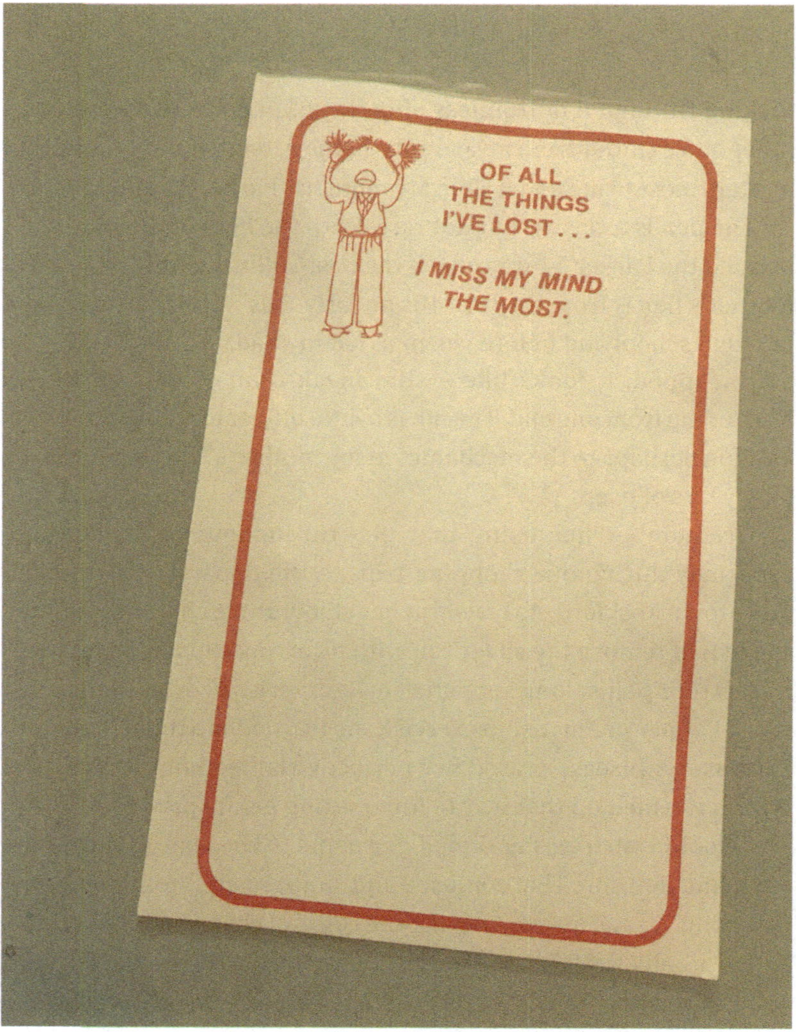
OF ALL
THE THINGS
I'VE LOST . . .
I MISS MY MIND
THE MOST.

JONI BLECHER

A pad is a strange thing to hold onto from childhood—especially, being the daughter of a printer. Paper was everywhere in our house.

At first, I liked the sketch of the girl squeezing her hair into two side ponytails. Maybe it was a boy. The character is wearing a vest and a tie. It was the '80s. Girls were sporting rainbow plaid ties.

I enjoyed decorating the outfit, sometimes drawing flowers on it and other times bathing it in a monochromatic ink pen blue. I noticed the red border next. The idea of a border on a plain old pad of paper was magical, like it was daring me to write a complete story within its confines.

When I saw the stack dwindled to two remaining pads, I grabbed them and buried them deep in a desk drawer. The thought of losing them filled me with dread.

Years later, I found the pads again. I saw past the image and finally noticed the text, "Of all the things I've lost... I miss my mind the most." Instantly, I knew why I kept them. That was my dad's sense of humor. He made the pad for fun because he could.

I still have the pad. A scant 10 sheets left. I only share it with people who will appreciate the pad's comedic relief or knew my dad. The pad reminds me to bring a little fun to everything I do... especially, if I'm losing my mind.

Storied Stuff

MARY B. HANSEN

When I was a child, my grandparents had these two magnets, among others, on their refrigerator door. For whatever reason, I was drawn to them and always looked for them when I came over to their house, like a touchstone. I particularly liked the one with the red nail polish. I maybe even coveted it a little.

When I was older, I learned the concept of tying a string around your finger to help you remember something. I think I even tried it once, but the string was annoying and I can't remember if it worked. What I do remember is being in their kitchen anticipating eating the cookies my grandmother just made or the leftover Mac and Cheese. She always asked, "What can I get you?" She showed her love with food.

My grandmother had a memory like a steel trap, recalling dates for small life events long forgotten by most. If there was a question about when something happened, she would be able to pull up the year quickly and with authority. She was always right. Until she wasn't.

As she aged into her late eighties, she lost her steel trap memory and became confused. Not even a string tied around her finger would help her as she was lost in her own mind. For me, that was the most heartbreaking part of her getting older; she couldn't remember what made her, *her*.

But I won't forget who she was, and I have the magnets to remind me.

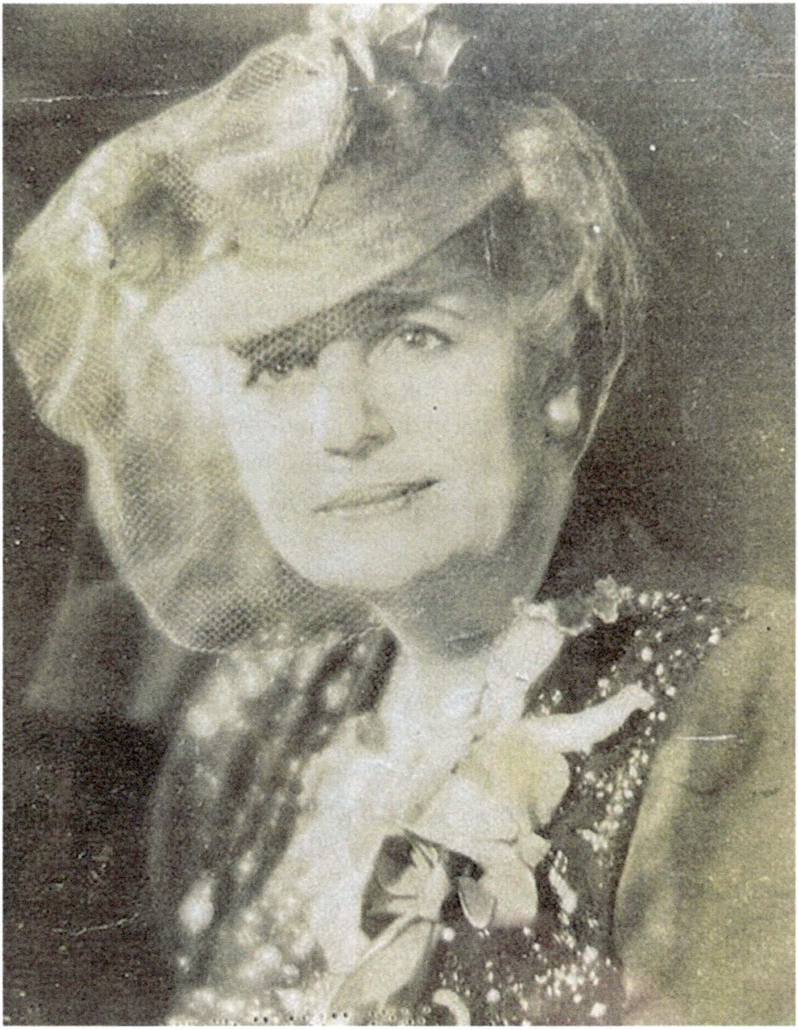

SUSAN GROUT

I have such fond memories of my Grandmother. Grandma Florence was a funny, controversial and rather well-padded figure who seriously attempted to instruct me in some of the home arts.

One time Grandma was trying to show me how to put a zipper in a dress while she was continually talking. With enthusiasm, she grabbed my rather shabby attempt at making an A line dress. All the while, she was trying to convince me that it was easy to install a zipper. *Zippp*! with the sewing machine as I watched with a degree of intimidation.

She stopped, cut the thread, whipped out the final product with a *voila*! Then she held her nose and started laughing uproariously. Grandma put the zipper in the dress not only upside down, but also backwards. We both laughed. That was the best lesson I ever had on not taking your mistakes so seriously.

Grandma Florence would send letters when I was away at college. I looked forward to her touching, almost apologetic letters and her efforts to encourage and connect with me. In many letters she'd include the contents of her coin purse and say, "Get yourself a chocolate soda!" This was her idea of the biggest treat. My roommates and I would laugh, getting a big charge out of Grandma.

I think of her often with laughter and miss her to this day. Now I know this is how I'd like to be remembered: with a wistful chuckle and a smile.

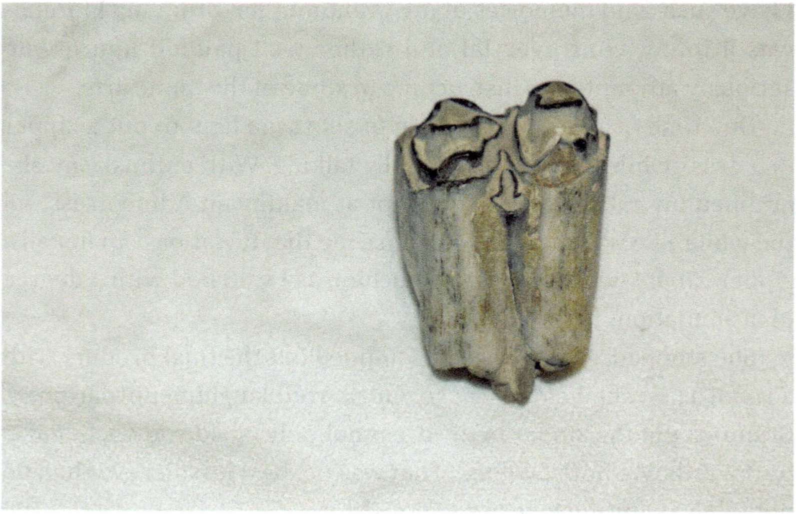

KATHY BRANT

Pelican Lake is one of the loveliest of Minnesota's 10,000 lakes, and it is where I spent one of the most delightful days of my childhood. My younger brother and I splashed through the water several docks down from where we were staying when we spied a school of tiny minnows. I stood very still, hoping to entice them to encircle my legs while my brother charged ahead.

It was then that I found it: a gray rock with curious blue ridges on top. When I turned it over, I saw four holes symmetrically spaced. A fossil! I screamed to my brother that I had found a dinosaur tooth. (What other kind of fossil is there?)

The rest of the day, adrenaline high, my brother and I searched for more teeth and bones, planning to build a dinosaur skeleton in our backyard, but we found nothing else. My mother took me and the tooth to the Geology department at North Dakota State University—it was called North Dakota Agricultural College then—and a kind professor took the time to look at a nine-year-old girl's treasure. He identified it as a fossilized bison or cow tooth. While disappointed it did not belong to a dinosaur, I loved that tooth and kept it hidden away in my room. Sometimes I would turn it over in my hands and remember the thrill of discovery and the magic of summer at the lake.

When I married and moved to Illinois, the tooth came with me. I keep it on a shelf in my living room alongside some art glass and a Royal Doulton figurine. Over the years it reminded me of the pure joy childhood can give and of home.

Now when I look at the tooth, it reminds me that days spent with my brother were finite. He left this world way too soon, and I so miss him.

Storied Stuff

WILLIAM ANTHONY

Hunkered down, here on the Maine coast, as in Boccaccio's *Decameron*, waiting for this new pestilence to pass, I commenced thinking about the glacier-scraped granite bedrock that lies beneath most of Maine. Its evidence is everywhere, if you look for it: the unforgiving rock ledges along Maine's jagged coast—the stone walls that wend their way along back roads and over old stone-stubbled pastures—here and there, the huge erratics left millennia ago by melting glaciers—and, after the summer people have left, when the sea turns gray as cold steel, there are the small stones I consider as I stroll Pemaquid Beach, lost in thought.

We humans stop to pick up beach stones for many reasons: we may take pleasure in a stone's shape or its color or perhaps we simply like the feel of a stone in our hand. But if I take a stone home, its beauty dims and the sea-soaked stone that was dark black when wet will dry out, lifeless. In time, I will forget whatever first drew my eyes to that stone and why I stopped to pluck that stone from the cold grasp of sand, crushed shells and seaweed, as if trying to rescue it from some anonymous fate.

The time-rounded sea-tossed beach stone in this photograph, sits on a piece of driftwood on the mantel over the fireplace in the cottage. It is a natural sculpture, a *memento mori*, millions of years old, that persists in this age of silicon impermanence and instant obsolescence. It is a reminder that my reflections on this stone's beauty are as ephemeral as a summer dragonfly. Soon enough I will again be but minerals and dust, this stone's distant relative.

Storied Stuff

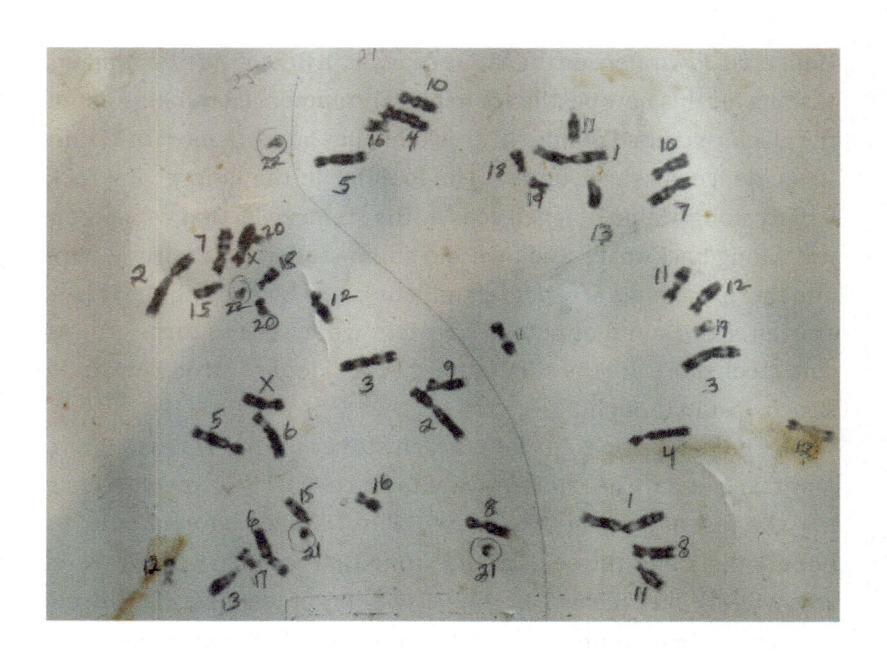

LIZA BLUE

These are mine and mine alone. My karyotype. Twenty-three pairs of my chromosomes spread across a slide I made when working in a cytogenics lab forty years ago. They have not changed since then, or before then.

In a professional karyotype the paired chromosomes with their characteristic banding are snipped out and arranged in order by size, from chromosome 1 to the X and Y sex chromosomes, like a police line-up. But I left my chromosomes where they lay splattered, after dropping them onto a slide.

The resulting picture has much more personality. As a group, the chromosomes look like an aerial view of dancers on a dance floor. At the center of the picture, chromosome 9 is cutting in on chromosome 2. Perhaps chromosomes 1 and 2, isolated at either side of the picture and obscured by a smear of blood, are desperately seeking each other.

My individuality is not visible from this level—that would require the identification of the individual genes resulting in the bar code that is a staple of *Law and Order SVU*. In fact my karyotype would not look any different from Hitler's or Mother Teresa's.

Regardless I see a distillation of my ancestors. The dour portraits of Henry and Nancy Farwell, my triple great grandparents, hang in my dining room. My genes may have gotten a bit dinged up through five generations and millions of divisions, but 1/32th of my karyotype can be traced back to each of these people. This karyotype is my constant.

Storied Stuff

LYNN BODNAR

My thoughts turned to my vintage gingerbread pan. Rich in tradition - it's from my great grandmother circa 1910. I imagined its travels and the hands it's passed through for over 100 years.

As my great grandmother mixed the ingredients, prepped the pan and baked the gingerbread, a certain essence of herself went into it. Imprinted into the pan. I can feel it. Perhaps during war times she was thrilled just to have the 1/3 cup of sugar needed. Other times may have brought easy gratitude, periods of angst, uncertainty, and surely the love of family through it all.

That same thread has been weaved through each subsequent owner of the pan, journeying through the generations. I'm inspired by and celebrate the women in my family history who came through it all and baked their way through it all—their strength to carry on, to provide, to bring forth comfort and joy.

Every year I also use the original handwritten recipe to enjoy this time-honored gingerbread tradition. It's ultimately about family - the love, the lives, the connection, the ribbon of DNA and the simple ingredients that all stream though this delicious act of honoring a family tradition.

I wish you could have a big warm slice, slathered in butter as you read this. But for now, I wish you connection to love and uplifting tradition that serves to warm your heart. Taking on the strength of those before us and being reminded of our own.

At the end of the recipe my great grandmother writes, "350 oven, 30 minutes. Never fails."

And it never does.

CREPES ROBERT

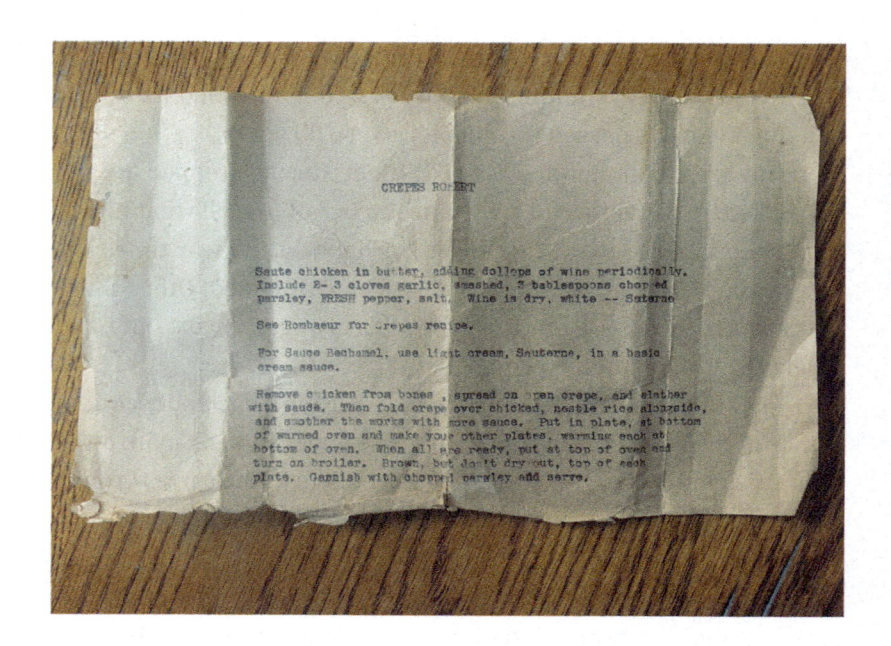

Saute chicken in butter, adding dollops of wine periodically. Include 2-3 cloves garlic, smashed, 3 tablespoons chopped parsley, FRESH pepper, salt. Wine is dry, white -- Saterne

See Rombaeur for crepes recipe.

For Sauce Bechamel, use light cream, Sauterne, in a basic cream sauce.

Remove chicken from bones, spread on open crepe, and slather with sauce. Then fold crepe over chicked, nestle rice alongside, and smother the works with more sauce. Put in plate, at bottom of warmed oven and make your other plates, warming each at bottom of oven. When all are ready, put at top of oven and turn on broiler. Brown, but don't dry out, top of each plate. Garnish with chopped parsley and serve.

PAT HITCHENS

Robert Hitchens' earliest meals came from his mother's pinched Depression-era larder in New Jersey. As a teenager, he shared uninspired but calorie-dense platters with farmhands in Kansas. It was not until the 1950s that he learned to *eat,* selling advertising for NBC Radio. Contracts were sealed with the aid of two-hour-plus business lunches along the bistro-packed blocks traversing New York's Manhattan Island – an international smorgasbord for client entertainment and the education of his palate.

I wonder about the first time Daddy furrowed bushy brows and looked a lunchtime chef in the eye. As a child I couldn't always decipher his intense expressions; what would a midday cook summoned to the dining room have expected? "This," I picture Daddy booming, finger pointing at the remains of *Boeuf-a-la-something,* adding with theatrical pause "– was superb! *Superb!*" What the client thought, I have no idea.

Soon after, I imagine Daddy following his reviews with follow-ups. "Is this browned under gas?" and "Where do pros buy cookware?" Commercial-grade sauté-pans began appearing at home, also carbon-steel knives and whisks. *The Joy of Cooking* acquired new spatters. Having learned to eat, Daddy would now *cook.*

Mother didn't mind; she found cooking boring – and my father had a gift! The kitchen was the boyhood chemistry set he never had; he loved sniffing spices or watching bubbling butter and flour joust in a pan. Mother favored Baroque kitchen music; my father whistled. She had measuring spoons; he trusted the palm of his hand.

"ROBERT" did not belong in Mother's recipe box. It offers no expertise in crepe-making, nor Bechamel, referring the reader elsewhere. Beyond "FRESH pepper," Daddy avoids inhibiting cooks, free to smash, slather, and smother – also fold, add dollops, even nestle – as interpreted.

CREPES ROBERT never tasted the same twice, but they were always good.

Storied Stuff

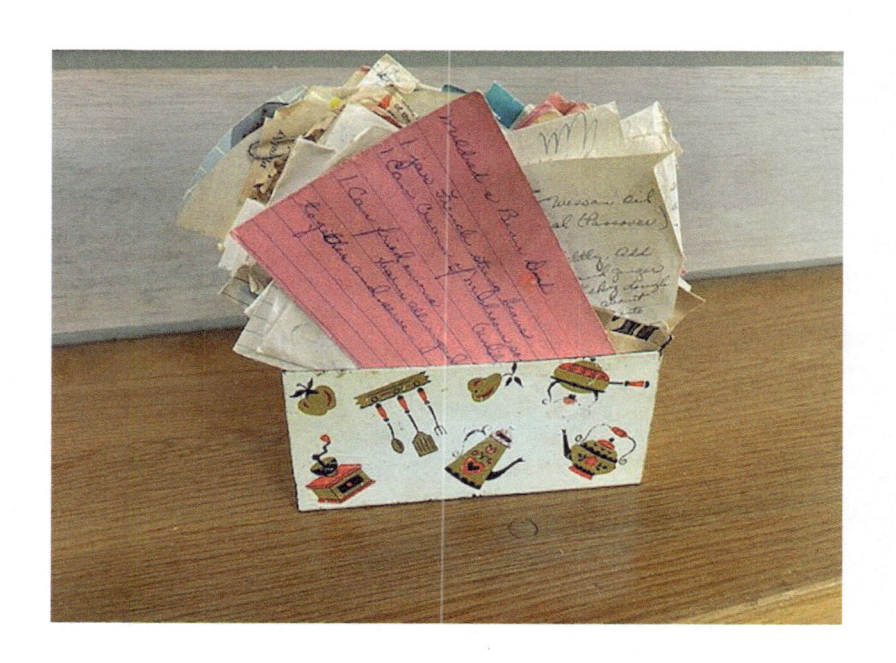

PAT KREGER

When my mother died, I inherited a few pieces of jewelry, her hand embroidered tablecloths, china and my prized possession, her recipe box. Mama was the classic Southern Jewish wife and mother of the Sixties. The breakfast table was always set the night before with cloth napkins, flatware and breakfast dishes; always lovely. Dinner included a first course. Remember pineapple rings with a scoop of cottage cheese, topped with a maraschino cherry?

Stuffed to overflowing, the recipe box is a treasure chest of daily and holiday recipes, a jumble of Sabbath dinner, Rosh Hashanah, Yom Kippur, Passover and Thanksgiving specialties gleaned from friends, relatives and magazines. How about Mildred's sweet and sour meatballs made with ketchup and grape jelly? Anyone up for brisket topped with Coca Cola and onion soup mix?

Family gathering meals always included noodle kugel and one of her new Jello mold recipes. My boys still make fun of me when I serve their Bubbie's unnaturally pink strawberry Jello mold. But everyone enjoys it and friends always want the recipe, which follows below. But what I love the most is reading the recipes in her beautiful, now fading, handwriting on the index cards. The recipe box reminds me of joyful family gatherings, Jello molds and all. But mostly, it reminds me of Mom.

Strawberry and Sour Cream Mold, Ruth Kreger

1 6-oz and 1 3-oz package strawberry Jello
Half the amount of water per standard recipe

2 small pkg frozen strawberries and juice (about 2 cups)
1 pt sour cream
Prepare concentrated Jello. Add sour cream and mix until Desired texture. Refrigerate.

Storied Stuff

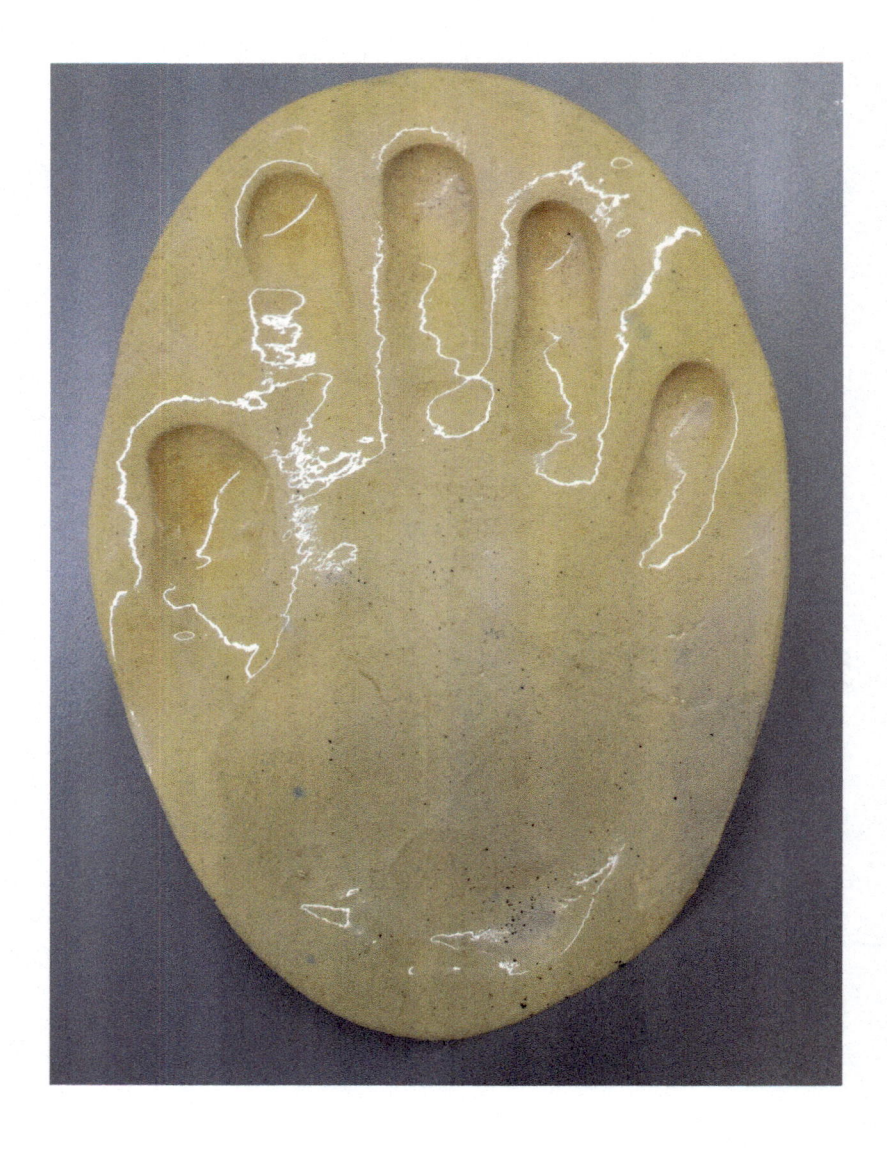

KEITH KRETCHMER

Five years old. I had been to pre-school. But going to South School for kindergarten was the big time. There were all kinds of fun things to play with—including a box with a giant steering wheel like a bus has—that captured my attention. I may have been a little clingy when my mom dropped me off, but Miss Steinke was warm and welcoming.

I don't remember much about daily activities then. Finger painting and other painting on easels, for sure. We had to bring one of our dad's old shirts to use as a smock. There was recess, of course. We had rest period each day on the rug. We also had a snack which often was Salerno butter cookies. We used to put them on our fingers and eat all of the bumps off the edge first before eating the rest of the cookie.

One day we had a project with clay. Each of us had a knob of clay which we flattened to about ½ inch thick. Then each of us stood up and made a handprint in the wet clay. Our teacher used a stylus to write my name on the underside of my piece, along with the month and year. Mine says "Keith Nov. 1956." It's an impression of my right hand. Once it dried or was fired (I don't remember) each of us painted our piece. Mine is yellow.

This memento sits on my bookshelf to this day. Do any of my classmates have theirs?

Storied Stuff

THOMAS G. FIFFER

Going to my father's office was a big deal. Not because he was a big deal attorney, but because I got time with him. Some Saturday mornings, he'd take me with for his "half-day," buckling me into his Mercedes 450SLC, the "fun car," which his mother called the "Mersa-deez" and considered a downgrade from the larger Cadillac that preceded it. The Cadillac was yellow, with white upholstery, and I insulted my dad when I called it a banana.

Down our street, Drexel "Ava-nyew," left on Vernon, right on Tower, then whizzing along Forest Way Drive's curves in a car engineered for speeds over 100 mph. Once on the highway, we reached the Loop quickly, passing through the tunnels my father called Big John and Little John as we neared the city.

His building, the Rookery, was the oldest skyscraper in Chicago with a soaring lobby (then plastered over) by Frank Lloyd Wright. His office was on the top floor, in the corner, and along with his king-size desk and elegant leather furniture were pictures of me and my brothers on the walls.

Not long before my father died, just after parking his Mercedes at my uncle's house with my mother and me inside, he let me use his office Xerox machine to make a copy of my hand. It's one of a handful of memories of direct interaction with him, lifting the cover, pressing my palm down on the glass, watching the paper emerge—like magic. Dad was an original.

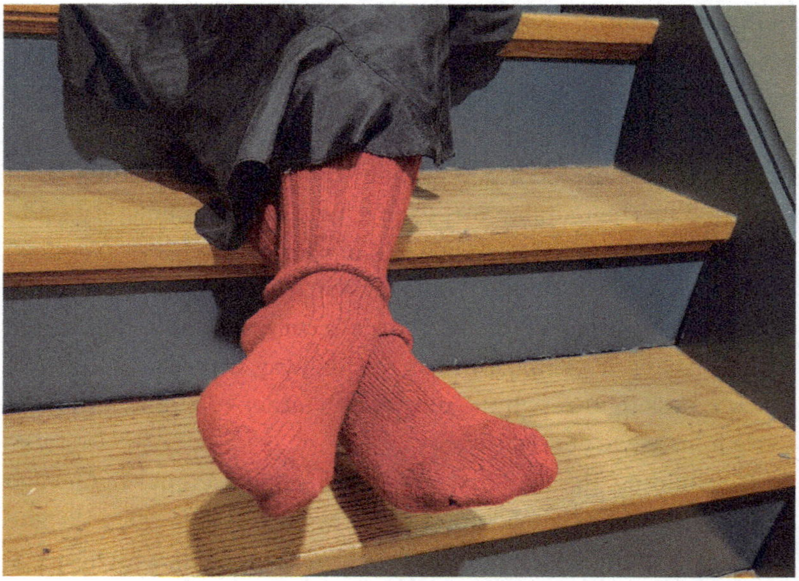

LAURIE KAHN

At eighty-one, after two heart attacks, my father announced he was going on a cruise. "Unwise," the doctors decreed, recalling his last heart attack that occurred while he vacationed on a remote Canadian island requiring a helicopter to take him to the nearest hospital. But my father stood firm. "If I die on the cruise, so be it. Let them throw me overboard."

The unwavering unrest between my mother and father allowed my father and me to have many adventures. My sister was my mother's companion, with an upside of visits to museums, theater, an introduction to classical music. The downside was endless struggles with my mother about her weight, her taste in clothes, and my sister's preference for white lipstick and teased hair.

I escaped my mother's tyranny of female expectations. My father and I went fishing, ate rare roast beef sandwiches slathered in coleslaw, cheered at football games, and endlessly talked politics.

My father, unlike my mother, was not taken with status or riches. My father's fishing philosophy was that we needed to rent an aluminum boat with a small motor and find the prettiest spot on the lake. He believed the fish simply would follow our lead.

On the third day of the cruise, my father had a heart attack and died. I have a picture on my nightstand taken the night before. He is sitting at the captain's table holding a glass of whiskey with his right hand lifted, making a toast. He is grinning. The morning before, I imagine he had two fried eggs, an order of greasy bacon followed by a cigarette that a swig of Coke may wash down. For my father, the battle between pleasure and longevity was no contest.

A week after he died, my sister and I met at my father's house in Florida. We rummaged through our father's clothes closet. With pride, he wore plaid pants with a striped shirt. My sister and I tried on my father's shirts, sweaters, and sport coats and giggled endlessly. My father was a great fan of humor and laughter and disliked any signs of melancholy. We opened the refrigerator door and found a half-eaten jar of guava jelly, cream cheese, and orange juice—the ideal snack.

We roamed around the house with a perfect pitch of irreverence.

Tasteful art, some bearing a signature, four antique chairs and a desk inherited from my grandparents, a set of polished silverware were a few of the treasures my sister and I ignored. Instead, we rummaged through the top drawer of my father's mahogany dresser and found the thing we both most wanted. Thank God there were two pairs of his red socks so we could both wear them to honor our father at his funeral.

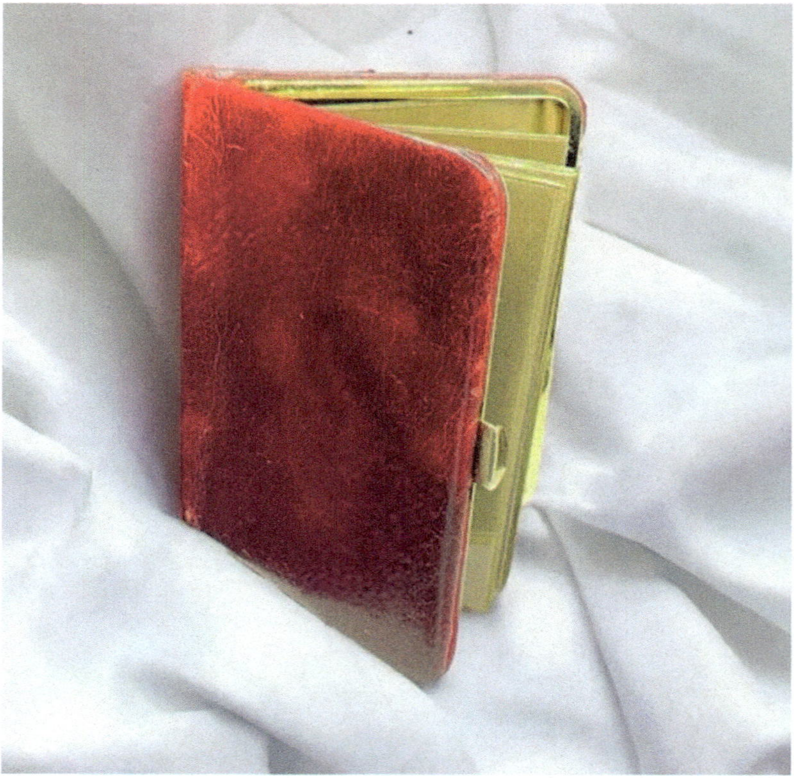

TUNI DEIGNAN

I can't not remember you, right? The relearning of our a, b, c's, the secrets you kept so cleverly inside, or
   fearfully,
   pocketed, in your purse.
   There was that small perfect photo keeper shaped like a deco fag case, gold-clip fasten, bound in cherry red leather,
   Smooth.
Cellophane slips with your dear ones shining through, 2 x 3 black and white mini-friezes, childhood besties Judith & Jeaner in cashmere and lipstick, Mary standing darkly against your father's Roadster in the driveway, her dress long to her shins, her arms crossed over her chest.
   Each of us four kids in all sorts of stages, infants bundled, one nursery aged and banged over eyebrows; Jordan, smart and turtlenecked, pants with pleats, wide-eyed, timid smile.
   You tucked us there like a love story amongst the tissues, the compact, the billfold. We were always only an unclip away.
   I never thought about that. So close. To your heart.
   "can I please,"
   "may I" you interrupted,
   "may I please look at the photo book mom?"
   So close. To your heart. You loved us; the red leather devotion.
   I can't not remember, I choose you differently now, refreshed, delicate, private, afraid,
   Precious.

Storied Stuff

ANNETTE GENDLER

Dad's photo albums stood on one of the upper shelves in Mom's living room wall cabinet. All eleven of them were rather small (7x9x1¼") and formed a solid block with their uniform dark green leather spines against the cabinet's light teak. In them, Dad had chronicled his life in the 1950s as an engineering student in Darmstadt, Germany—before he shipped off to the US on a Fulbright Scholarship to get his PhD at Purdue, before he knew Mom, and before any of us kids entered his life.

I took them down and looked through them again last March, when my sister and I were cleaning out Mom's old apartment, a task that felt odd, as Mom was still alive. However, in her advanced stage of dementia, most of her belongings confused her or meant nothing to her anymore. Being alone in her apartment had become unbearable to her, so the week before we had moved her into a group home for seniors with dementia.

What a delight to leaf through Dad's beautifully arranged pages! He had assembled them the way his parents had always done their photo albums: black and white photographs, printed on high quality paper, their white frames trimmed with curlicue scissors to create decorative edges, laid out on black album paper, captions calligraphed in white ink. Ticket stubs from plays or exhibitions, particularly tech fairs, as well as postcards from trips added variety. There were pictures from travels with friends, snapshots of laboratory work settings, portraits of himself and his parents—all well composed and not a single one out of focus.

Here and there, I found that Mom had written into the albums with a ballpoint pen. Trying to make sense of them, she had scribbled notes on some pages or had written the year the album encapsulated on the inside cover, '57, even though it was indicated elsewhere. I loved her handwriting, but not here.

Then, suddenly, I came upon a spread, where, through the glassine interleaf, an empty page with bits of glue, traces of paper stuck to them, gaped at me. What was this? As I paged along, I discovered more instances where photos had been ripped out.

"What happened?" I asked my sister, holding up a violated double page.

"Yeah," my sister sighed, "I saw that when I looked at the albums a while back. Apparently, Mom tore out pictures. Who knows why or where they are."

Our dad passed away 37 years ago. If he had removed pictures, he would have carefully pried them off, sliding a penknife between photo and paper, aiming to leave no trace. Instead, we were left with these destroyed pages, this collision of Mom's confusion later in life and Dad's care and competency in visual presentation.

HAROLD SCHIMMEL
HAROLD SCHIMMEL
GERSHOM SCHOLEM
DENNIS SILK

JOANNA CLAPPS HERMAN

Unpacking 20 boxes of books that I had stored for eight years after my husband, Bill, died and I'd had to move, I found my small leather atlas—about 6 X 5. It's the kind of thing I coveted with such lust when I came upon it in a store of maps and globes that on an impulse, I'd bought it knowing it was way too expensive. But in that moment, it seemed as if owning that one small leather-bound atlas would confer upon me a library with good deep reading chairs, a fine immense desk, perfect lamps, an expensive slightly worn rug.

There was also a fireplace and a window that looked out on my garden, rather than the one-bedroom apartment where I actually live in Harlem with my single table that is dining, prep table and desk. I rarely open that atlas, even now, but when I came upon it along with six copies of *War and Peace*, all my other books, Bill's dissertation, his marked-up *Ulysses*, I felt the same thrill of my leather beauty. It's so compact and it holds the whole world and the many places I'll never get to see.

Storied Stuff

MARK LARSON

I learned to read in school. I learned to *want* to read by watching my father. He journeyed through his world ruddered by a ceaseless succession of books. He identified points of interest along the way with his busy underlining pen, markers that I would later follow. I see him standing before his bookshelf, surveying it like a plot of land he owned. Then he'd slide a book out of its place, leaving a gap like the one between his front teeth, and open it.

I was 11 when we moved from Park Ridge to Evanston, where I didn't know a single soul. One Saturday morning, unbeknownst to anyone, my younger brother, Brad, and I returned by bike. We arrived in Park Ridge seven hours later, filthy and spent. My displeased father drove us back to Evanston.

That night, he set on my bed a red book titled, *The Greatest Thing Since Sliced Bread*. It was about a 9-year-old boy who, with his younger sister, makes a pilgrimage across town to visit a friend who had moved away.

It was the first book of its length that I'd read, and my first experience with *I'll-just-read-one-more-chapter-before-I-sleep*. That book has stood on every bookshelf throughout my life.

My father died on February 25th, 2020. That night, I stood before his bookshelf. I found a copy of a book I had recently published. I slid it out, leaving a gap like the one between my front teeth. Opened it. And my eyes fell to his underscores, which marked his journey through *my* life.

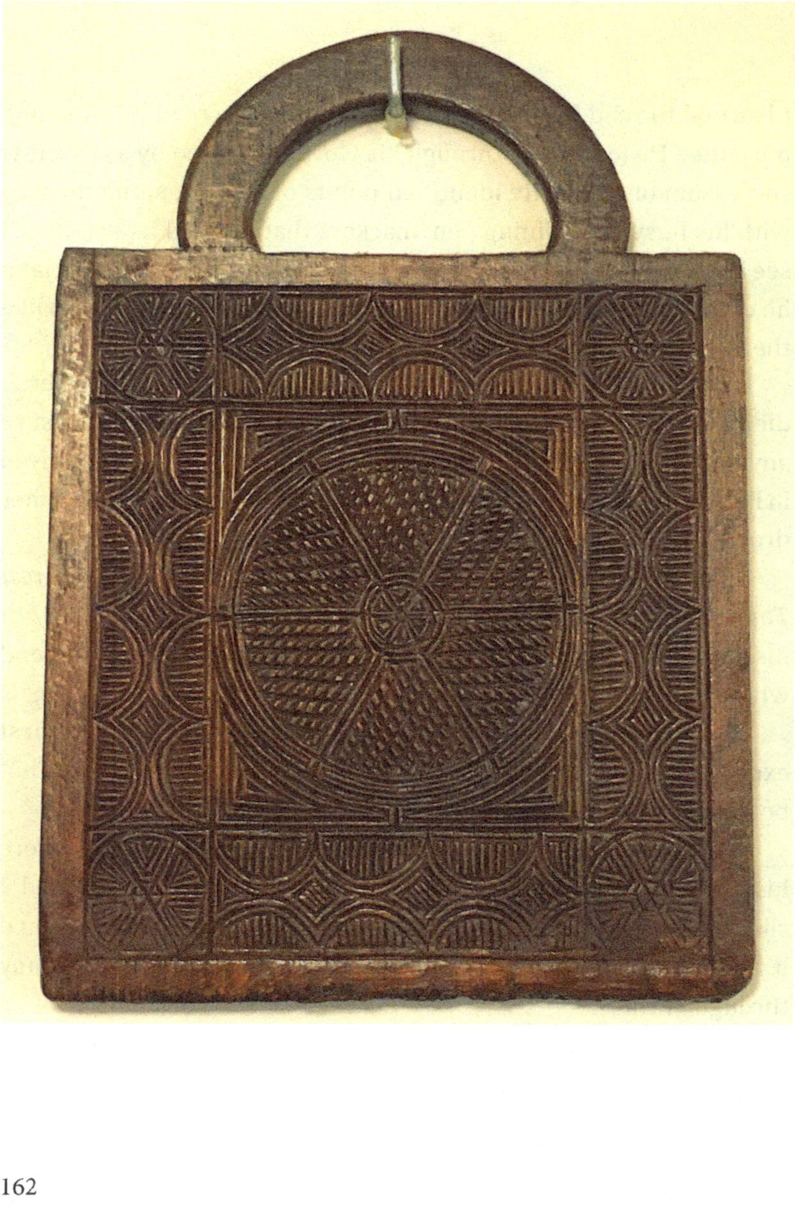

KATHLEEN CAPRARIO-ULRICH

A humble item.

My newlywed grandparents, Pasquale and Donata Maria Caprario, left the Italian hill country east of Naples for a new beginning and the children they imagined they'd share it with. They traveled across the broad and tumultuous Atlantic in steerage and arrived at Ellis Island, New York, on May 10, 1902.

Story has it, my grandfather was so ill when they disembarked that he was held for observation with a red "X" drawn on his back signifying possible deportation. After several days he recovered and was released into the care of his older brother who'd immigrated seven years earlier and was their sponsor.

Turns out, my grandfather suffered from severe dehydration as a result of non-stop seasickness while in transit and not tuberculosis. Some honeymoon. My grandparents settled in Elizabeth, New Jersey, where they raised three American-born children, one of whom was my dad.

An intricately-carved breadboard accompanied them across that gut-turning ocean. It must have held great importance to have been included along with their hopes and dreams in the one tiny trunk they brought with them, the size of a small carry-on. Perhaps it was a wedding gift or a gently-used item given them so as never to forget where they'd come from or those they left behind. I don't know. That wasn't part of the story.

The breadboard's cutting side is heavily marked and a testament to the hundreds of loaves of bread sliced on its surface that nourished their family. It now hangs on my wall where it reminds me of the sacrifices my grandparents made as first-generation immigrants and the aspirations that fueled their relentless desire for a better life for themselves and their children.

For me.

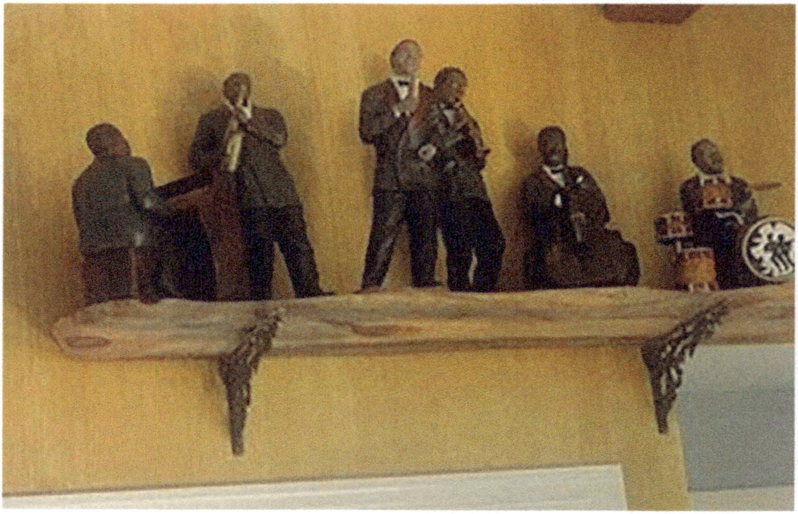

INA CHADWICK

Though the joint ain't officially open, this combo is our very own Jazz band straight from Hudson, NY, where I found them in a parking lot pop-up vintage sale.

It was the Saturday right after the fiscal crisis hit in 2008, and it was my husband's birthday. He's a musician. And a dentist part of the time, too.

I actually bargained with owner, who was asking $2500. I'd never bargained before, but I was able to take the guys in the band home for $1400.

We put them on the top of a stairway landing. They're composite and so very retro 1950s bar window decorations. We even bought a Louis Armstrong Jazz at Radio Station WNEW poster to hang over them.

When we began a renovation that repurposed my husband's dental home office—he'd moved locations— we had the back wall in what we now call "the West Wing" faux-painted. We then created a "bandstand," using a piece of live edge wood my husband found at Monger's Market, a salvage warehouse in Bridgeport, and wrought iron brackets that had belonged to my mother before being relegated to our basement.

At last it was showtime. And it remains so these many years later. We've got ourselves a house band. And I swear, I can almost hear them when the lights go down.

Storied Stuff

SUZANNE GUESS

In fourth grade, my music teacher recommended that I learn to play an instrument after I did well on the flutophone (a white plastic tube with red keys that looked like a recorder) music unit. I chose the flute after being entranced by it during an elementary school concert when I was in first grade. It had been a long three-year wait.

I went all in on music education: summer band camp, marching across football fields and down streets in parade formation, and earning college credits for playing in a wind ensemble. After college, I put my flute away and did not play it again for 20 years until a friend from elementary school encouraged me to join the community band where he played. "No, I said, "it's been too long."

"It's like riding a bike," he told me. "You don't forget"

He was partially right, because I did forget that key signatures aren't suggestions, the necessary air pressure to hit a third octave B-flat, and the trills that sound like what hummingbird wings look like when the birds go in for the sugar water.

I've been playing in a community band for several years now, and it's a joy to share key signature fails, accidental solos, friendship, and bad jokes with those who come together for a single reason: to play music. It provides a small measure of healing to create something beautiful in a world where polarization is the norm, students are shot dead at school, and the earth warms as a consequence of our actions.

I think of the girl I first saw playing a flute in the elementary school band, and I hope that she is still playing her flute, too.

Storied Stuff

JUDY IACUZZI

An instrument in the history of our family and still in our living room in Evanston today is the mahogany upright piano made by Acrosonic. It first occupied one wall of the living room of my childhood home in Ohio. Today badly in need of tuning, then it acceded to the playful chords of my brother, sister and me, and occasionally friends who dropped in. My lessons started in first grade and continued through high school. My teacher, Frieda Schumacher, came to our wedding, and the duets my best friend and I played in recitals in middle school orchestrated an abiding friendship to this day.

But there are two piano notables back then I write about now. My grandfather, "Gaga," and a good friend of the family, "Aunt" Jo Foltz. Because it was these two and their love of us and the piano that spurred me to continue the agony of practicing day after day for years of my childhood.

Gaga's applause I can still hear, some 60 years after his death. Practice time after school and he'd be there in the wooden chair beside the piano bench commenting in his special way. Five claps for a perfect rendition, four for one or two mistakes and three for something that needed practice. As much as I worked the piece ahead of time, I listened for his applause at the end. This was our routine — one that began in first grade and ended only when he no longer could drive to our home.

His friend and our family friend was Jo from Memphis. A few times a year she would visit the North because her son's family lived in Cleveland. And if we were lucky, she would come to our home for supper. She had perfect pitch, a throaty voice, a luminous face and golden hair swept into a French twist. She made the Acrosonic sing and drew the tone deaf to its keyboard. At five and six years old, I would join the group in our living room, hugging close to the talented lady on the bench, watching her hands, her ruby fingernails, her shoulders pumping with the pauses and starts of the music she played by ear.

I loved these evenings and hated it when my folks called it a day. But Aunt Jo would indulge me. What song did I want to hear as I was dragged upstairs to bed? My choice was always the same, and I thrilled as the percussive notes of "The Birth of the Blues" swirled up the stairs and into my room. I could hear the partygoers downstairs singing along with Jo and me,

And then they nursed it, rehearsed it
And sent out the news
That the Southland gave birth to the blues!

I still hear them. Gaga with his deliberate clapping, Jo performing like nobody else.

Perhaps I'll get it tuned and nurse it again...for some musical child in need of encouragement or a keyboard lullaby.

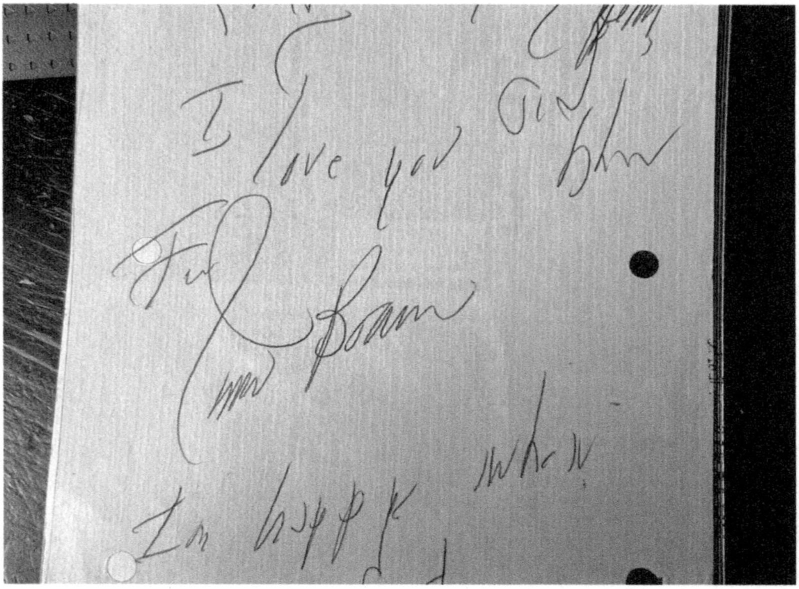
I love you

LISA LAUREN

You look at me and think: *This woman is clearly not Black. She is probably not that soulful.* But if I told you that this woman played the piano with James Brown, yep, James Brown, the one and only high-octane performer who sang songs like "I Feel Good", "Get On Up," and "Santa, Go Straight to the Ghetto," you would probably have a hard time believing me. But it did happen.

Around 11 am one Saturday afternoon circa 1987, I was in the lobby of the Hotel Nikko Chicago, playing my steady solo piano gig. James Brown wandered in with a few of his entourage milling about nearby. There I sat, playing some dreamy jazz standard, when I realized he was coming towards me. I often try to remember what was going through my mind during those seconds as he approached me. I'm sure it was an overwhelming feeling of surreal disbelief, a full body cringe anticipating what was to happen next.

Before I knew it, he was next to me at the piano saying, "Let's do a song together!" My brain scanned through my repertoire; there was nowhere to stop. I didn't have anything particularly funky or soulful at my fingertips, certainly nothing on the order of "Papa's Got A Brand New Bag."

Somehow my brain landed on "It Had to Be You" (which now seems utterly ridiculous), and moments later, James Brown and I were performing together. This man known for his raucous and flashy performances was sweetly singing a jazz standard a heartbeat away from me. My heart was racing the whole time, and my mind was knocking around the possibility that this might just be a dream, and when I woke up and described the dream to someone, they would chuckle and change the subject.

The funny thing was, there was almost no traffic in the lobby, so our little show was, under James Brown circumstances, very poorly attended. Amazingly, he wanted to continue. Was there any way I could have studied FUNK piano in my early years of training which would have prepared me for this moment? Having to decide quickly, I made another random selection: "I've Got You Under My Skin."

Miraculously, after that tepid choice of a decidedly white society song, he wanted to do one more. Finally, a tune came to mind with a little more soul: "Georgia." He ripped through the number, and I gave my lame-best attempt to come remotely close to his level. I don't think I got there, but it was still an unforgettable high. After our unrehearsed program was over, he gave me a big hug and I worried that his heavy makeup might get on my clothes.

Mr. Brown made his exit, and afterwards I played a few more tunes just to prove to anyone who happened to be around that I was a professional and could easily launch into a Rodgers and Hart number after having just played with the Minister of Super Heavy Funk. In my *pinch-me-now*, other-worldly state of mind, it didn't occur to me until much later that this was most likely THE most low-key performance of James Brown's career.

When it was time to take a break, I ran to the phone and called the first person I thought would appreciate my recent acclaim. "Mom, you'll never believe who I just played with!" I quietly shrieked into the hotel phone booth. "Who?" she said calmly, probably while playing solitaire. "The Godfather of Soul!"

Her reply (rather disappointing considering the magnitude of James' celebrity) was, "Don't make me guess." Well, my mom DID know who James Brown was, even if she didn't know his official title, and was eventually quite impressed - as any mom would be - with my story.

Since this scene had taken place before the days of cell phones, there was no way to document such an event, unless you happened to have a camera handy. So in a desperate attempt to memorialize the occasion I had asked him to sign my music. He scribbled, "Lisa, I love you. From James Brown. I'm happy when I meet my sweet Lorraine." Not sure where that last part came from - maybe I reminded him of someone named Lorraine. Or Nat King Cole. Or the drugs were wearing off. It didn't matter. I loved him, too.

SHORTEST WAY HOME

For Fred Kroeger,
A trailblazer who made it a little easier for those who follow your path,

FRED KARGER

In 2010, after a quarter century as a political consultant and half a dozen years as a political activist, I decided to run for president. Besides the fact that I'd never held elected office; would be the first openly gay person to seek a major party nomination; and was running as a moderate, pro-choice, Republican; it seemed destined to be a cakewalk.

Seriously, though, despite knowing I had zero chance of being the Republican nominee in 2012, there was a method to my madness. Contemplating my run, I took inspiration from one of my heroes, Shirley Chisholm, the first African American woman to serve in Congress and, in 1972, the first African American in a major party to run for President of the United States. She later explained: "I ran for the presidency, despite hopeless odds, to demonstrate the sheer will and refusal to accept the status quo. The next time a woman runs, or a black, a Jew, or anyone from a group that the country is 'not ready' to elect to its highest office, I believe that he or she will be taken seriously from the start."

I wanted the next generation to see firsthand that it was possible for a gay man or woman to seek the highest elected office in the land… and be taken seriously while doing so. That dream came to pass last year in the person of the remarkable Pete Buttigieg. Although Pete did not win, he was certainly taken seriously. Just as I hope my candidacy made it a little easier for him to run, his candidacy will make it a lot easier for others from the LBGTQ community to run in the future.

I met Pete for the first time in February 2019. I had a copy of his autobiography with me and asked him to sign it. His words make the book one of my prized possessions: "For Fred Karger: A trailblazer who made it a little easier to those who follow your path."

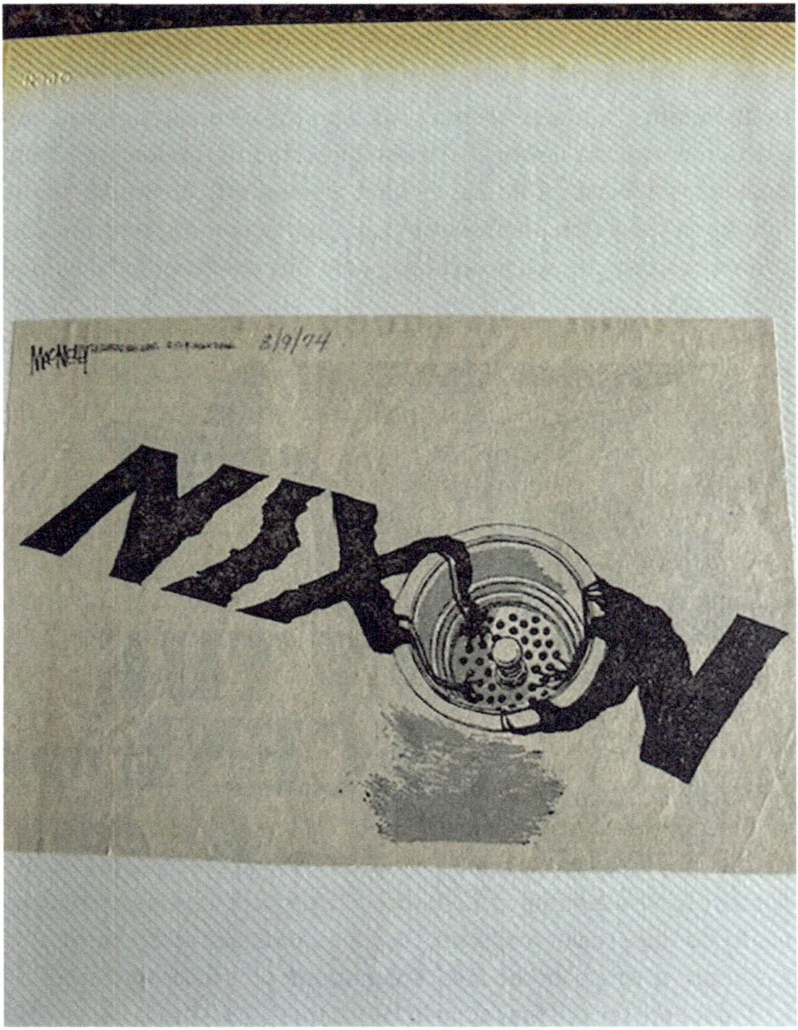
8/9/74
NIXON

VALERIE KRETCHMER

It was the summer of 1974, and I had just graduated from college. I was consumed with the Watergate hearings, as were many of us that summer. I devoured the local Chicago newspapers and listened to the hearings every day. No internet in those days to read the out-of-town papers online, just the *Tribune* and *Sun-Times*.

I became intrigued by the political cartoons that appeared each day and started clipping ones I thought were especially insightful, clever, and piercing. This was the start of my political cartoon collection that continues to this day. I have albums filled with cartoons I considered to be "collection worthy," meaning they withstand the test of time. They are a different and often irreverent take on history.

Even after 50 years, my all-time favorite is this one that ran the day after Nixon resigned on August 8, 1974. I love the idea of Nixon going down the drain. So simple, but so effective at communicating this historic event. That's what makes this and the others in my collection so special.

Storied Stuff

FRED GANTS

To quote from a skit on *Saturday Night Live*: "Baseball been berry berry good to me." My infatuation with America's Pastime began in 1957, when I went to my first game with my dad at the original Yankee Stadium. Walking to the mezzanine I looked down on the fans on the lower deck that led to a beautiful green field in urban Bronx. My dad bought me a scorecard and pencil and taught me how to score.

In 1962, I attended my first game at the Polo Grounds in Upper Manhattan, with the Mets—in their very first year—hosting my then favorite team, the Dodgers. At this ballpark, which had stood empty after the baseball Giants departed New York for San Francisco in 1957, I watched legendary players Willie Mays, Duke Snider, and Sandy Koufax, who gained my affection for refusing to pitch in the World Series on Yom Kippur.

In the mid-1960s in Westchester County, where I played youth baseball, the real star was my late brother. Ralph was a great Little League pitcher for the champion Mamaroneck Fire Department Foxes and hit several home runs. Years later I watched him hit a walk-off double down the right field line to give Mamaroneck High School the win over New Rochelle with Willie Mays Jr. in the outfield.

In the late '70s, while living in Madison, WI, I started a tradition of going to Wrigley Field with friends to see the Dodgers play the Cubs. Over the years, "Dodger Day" grew to 50 tickets and pictures with Ernie Banks, Bill Buckner (who later made an error causing the Red Sox to lose a World Series to the Mets), and Tom Lasorda.

On my wedding day in 1984, Jack Morris of the Tigers threw a no-hitter, and my friends held up baseball bats that my bride and I walked under. Ten years later, our family's Christmas card featured our three sons in their baseball uniforms. In 2014—on the day he was sworn in as Chief Justice of the Massachusetts Supreme Judicial Court—my brother Ralph threw out the first ball at Fenway Park.

To commemorate my relationship with baseball, my wife Tracy put together this pictured shrine, Including the photo of Ralph at Fenway, a Christmas card of my ball playing sons, a baseball bat mirror and autographed baseballs of Duke Snider, Bob Feller, and Tom Lasorda.

It's a berry berry good testament to a lifelong love of baseball, fields, and my now favorite Brewers at Milwaukee County Stadium and Miller Park, this year aptly known for the first time as American Family Field.

America's Smartest Theatre Restaurant presenting spectacolor revues, and dancing to two famous orchestras amidst an atmosphere of pageantry and splendor. Spend "An Evening in Paris" and see Paris, "City of Light," in all its magnificent beauty.
"An Evening in Paris"
The Exclusive Gold Key Club
EVENING'S ENTERTAINMENT
COURSE DINNER
SHOW DANCING
$5.95
3¢
STAMP
U.S.A.
POSTAGE
Giant Post Card
To Bobby
Best Wishes
Stan Musial
Chez Paree
CHICAGO

BOB KAUFMAN

Kick back. Pour yourself a scotch, or a straight up martini with a pimento stuffed olive, long before blue cheese was the rage. Crank up the hi-fi, and play some swing, or some jazz. Take yourself back to the days when ballplayers would come through town to play during the day at Wrigley or Comiskey, and then play at night on Rush Street or, in this case, the Chez Paree.

That is where my dad approached Del Ennis of the Cardinals, and his more widely known teammate Stan. As in, The Man. Both of whom graciously signed the "Giant Post Card" you see.

Back to the days when the best athletes were known only by their first names. Oscar, Elgin and Jerry on the hardcourt, Arnie and Jack on the tee, and Stan, Hank, Ernie, Mickey and Yogi on the ballfield. No last names needed for the best.

And how appropriate that it was at the Chez Paree, where the bottom of the card says you could get a 5 course dinner, after dinner liqueur, a show and dancing for $5.95 ("plus tax").

And what a show it must have been. The reverse side of the Giant Post Card (which you could mail with a 3 cent stamp) shows hundreds of the faces of the singers and comedians who performed on that stage. And, not unlike Stan, the best were recognizable only by their first names—Sammy, Nat, Dean, Milton, Cab, Duke and Frank.

The other first name on the card? That would be mine. It is what makes this Giant Post Card rather special.

So, kick back. Pour yourself a scotch, or a straight up martini with a pimento stuffed olive. Crank up the hi-fi, and play some swing, or some jazz. Take yourself back to the days.

Storied Stuff

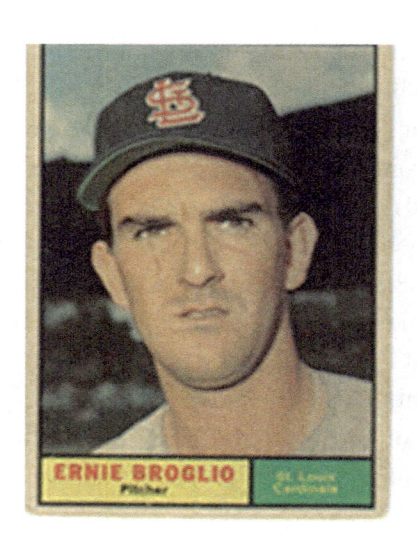

ROBERT J. ELISBERG

Far too many young men have returned home to get their childhood collection of baseball cards, only to find that their mother threw them out years earlier. (Or worse, *months* earlier.)

Happily, I come from good stock, and my mother always kept them. And I still have them—all 1,333. They're not as valuable as they could be – not in pristine condition. But that's because I actually played with them. (What a concept, I know.) Mainly, I invented a game called Dice Baseball, for which the stats on the back were integral.

There's definitely some value to the collection – especially my most valuable, a 1960 rookie card for Hall of Famer Carl Yastrzemski of the Boston Red Sox. Though the one that makes me most wistful is pitcher Tom Qualters – I have *eight* cards for him! If he had been in the Hall of Fame, as well, I could have retired decades ago. Alas, his 3-year record was 0-0 with a 5.64 ERA. According to Wikipedia, "He is the only pitcher to appear on a Topps baseball card four times without ever recording a win or loss."

But then there are my two most memorable cards.

"Brock for Broglio" is a cry Cubs fans have bemoaned since the middle of 1964. That's when the team traded their young, promising outfielder to the St. Louis Cardinals for Ernie Broglio, a journeyman pitcher. Broglio played only two seasons after that, winning just 12 games for the Cubs. That young outfielder, Lou Brock, went on to a Hall of Fame career and retired with the most stolen bases in major league history.

Not only do I have a card for both players – I have Ernie Broglio gratefully back on the Cardinals, and Lou Brock still blessedly on the Cubs. Where he has remained in my heart.

Storied Stuff

ALLYSON DYKHUIZEN

Jason Hanson was the one consistent shining light through the darkness that was being a Detroit Lions fan throughout my childhood and into adulthood. He played his entire 21-year career as kicker for the Lions, and whenever those truly horrible teams got anywhere near field goal range he got them 3 points! So the final score would be 24-3 and not 24-0.

In 2007 I was living in Chicago and got a pity invite to join my office fantasy football league AND WON! My Chicago Bears fan coworkers found a Jason Hanson trading card to give me with my cash reward, probably as a joke—but the joke was on them because I loved that thing. I taped it next to my desk where it lived until I left that job to start my own business. Seeing Jason every day was a reminder that I can do anything I put my mind to, and that being the underdog is a powerful motivator.

After a few moves that card got tucked here or there and hadn't been seen in a long time, but I thought about it a lot last season when the Lions made it to the NFC Championship Game. Before last season it was such a weird choice to be a Lions fan, and then all of a sudden all of these other Michigan transplants were everywhere, wearing their Lions hats and sweatshirts! We'd lock eyes on the street like, "WE DID IT!"

Digging through that Stuff You Don't Know What To Do With Cabinet recently, under old tax filings and years of birthday cards, I finally unearthed my checkbook and safely tucked inside there it was! A Topps Fantasports Jason Hanson Lions card from 1993. "Jason Hanson," the card reads, "drafted in the second round by the Detroit Lions last year, did not disappoint the Silverdome fans," SILVERDOME! Be still my HEART! "going 15 for 15 from inside the 45-yard line."

Casting my checkbook aside I quickly restored that card to its rightful place of prominence near my desk, next to my grandfather's obituary (who died during a season the Lions only won 6 games), on top of a picture from my wedding. Welcome back, Jason!

Storied Stuff

JOSH KAPLAN

When I was in college, a woman who lived off-campus, a former college librarian, befriended me, just as she had done with many of the kids at the college over the years. She was in her mid-80s when we met, and Dacie Moses was her name—Dacie being a nickname for Candace.

Her home, just off campus, was an oasis, a place to play a game of cribbage and to just get away from dorm life for a while.

One day I asked her if I could have a cutting from her massive Christmas cactus. She happily agreed, but told me that I had to promise to take good care of it for the rest of my life. I assented, gladly. Dacie went on to say that her plant was given to her by her father, who was given it, "as the war was winding down before I was born."

At that moment I did not think about what she was saying, but a couple of days later I asked her about "the war." I asked her if her dad was in WWI. She laughed and repeated that her dad had been in war before she'd even been born.

I cocked my head, and she smiled. "Yes, he got this plant at the end of the Civil War."

I have watched over and loved my Civil War cactus ever since. Every year, at Easter (I don't know why), it blooms. And I think of Dacie.

Storied Stuff

BETSY LACKEY

This is my mother's dieffenbachia. She probably got it when I was in 6-7th grade, which means it's almost 60 years old. Periodically it would get "leggy" and she would cut it back, put the leaves in water and cut the stalk to start a new plant. Then she would share the new plants with her friends and family. I inherited this plant in 2010, and now, once again, it has gotten "leggy." So, today I cut it back.

In addition to being a "mother" to many, many dieffenbachias passed out all over southeast Michigan, this plant has had its share of near-death experiences – from travelling in the back of the car to a new location to almost being eaten by the cat. However, this plant's most harrowing experience came one summer when my mother's aunt, my Great-Aunt Pauline, was staying with her. Somehow, the plant developed an infestation of tiny flies. It took my mother and my great-aunt several days to figure out where these tiny little critters were coming from. The minute they figured it out Pauline sprang into action. Luckily (?) my mother had just purchased some potting soil, so Pauline pulled the dieffenbachia out of the pot, threw all the soil away, washed the pot completely———(makes sense so far)

And then knocked all the soil off the roots and washed the roots and plant and all in soapy water.

Then she repotted the plant. As you can see, it survived.

Storied Stuff

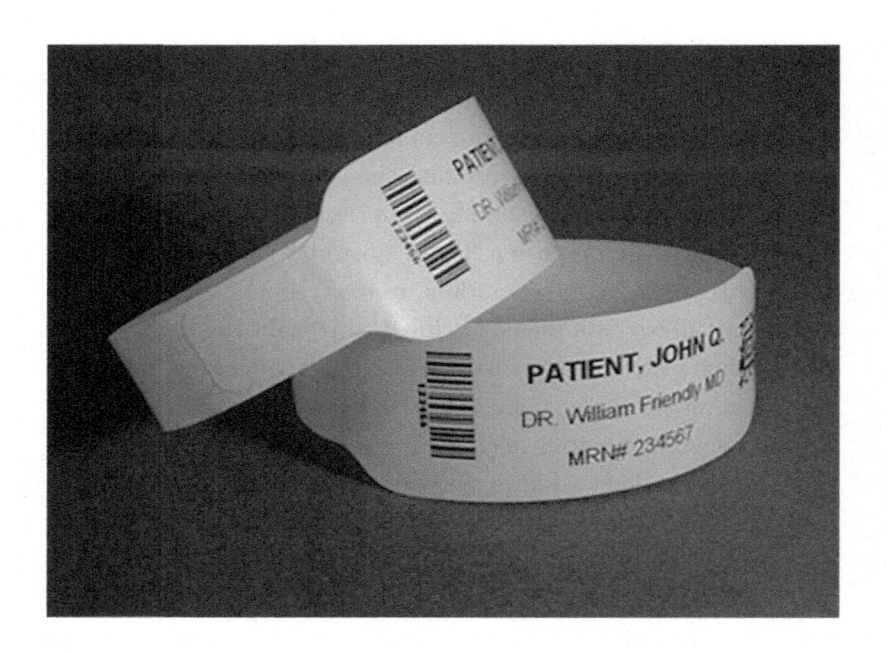

ELIZABETH DRUCKER

After sporting so many plastic hospital bracelets, it's hard to think of myself as anything other than a career mental patient. They may show my name and medical record number, but they reveal nothing about my story: what I did *this* time, what led to my being swept through yet another set of locked doors and their unbreakable glass windows. They are always loose, but not enough that I could just slide them around the bones of my wrist and off my hands.

These hospital bracelets remind everyone that I am sick. I am hopelessly bipolar, so it's anyone's guess what sort of mood state has gotten me in trouble this time. Sometimes, I take an Uber to the Emergency Room because I am hopelessly depressed and terrified that I might do something about it. Other times, I have been brought to the hospital by an assortment of well-intentioned friends who miss the old Elizabeth.

But, to me, my hospital bracelets remind me of my humanity, that despite everything I am going through, I still exist. As a person. My name is in bold print, capital letters, undeniable and floridly beautiful in its own way. *I can't be a patient forever*, I tell myself as I drift off to sleep in my hospital bed each night.

I look at my hospital bracelets during morning rounds when the treatment team reminds me that I am so ill that I might need to spend another week in the hospital, that I will probably have to take a medical withdrawal from school.

Whenever I feel panicky or uncertain during my hospitalizations, these plastic bands ground me. It doesn't really matter what put me in the psych ward or what I need to do to get discharged. My hospital bracelets provide me with the most beautiful thing any doctor could tell me: *I really do exist.*

Storied Stuff

JEAN HARNED BOYLE

For Christmas, when I was around 10 years old, my aunt gave me and my sister silver charm bracelets. To my bracelet she had added a silver horse charm because I was totally obsessed with animals, especially horses.

Over the years I got charms as gifts for birthdays, Christmas and other special occasions. On family camping trips around the country, my sister and I spent a great deal of time looking through souvenir shops for the perfect charms to represent each significant location.

To these I added charms for the different places I lived, schools I went to, and then, what I thought was my final "growing up" charm, the completion of the bracelet, a Hansom Cab, given to me by my now husband to remind me of our first date in New York City.

Years passed, many years, and I got the biggest surprise of my life – I had a granddaughter! My son had died 20 years earlier at the age of 24. He never knew that he had a daughter and she didn't know about her biological father until shortly before seeking me out just before her 24th birthday. My son and granddaughter were both born in August so I added the final charm, a beautiful little peridot stone.

My childhood charm bracelet will always be one of my most loved possessions. Today it hangs around the neck of a crow, on my fireplace mantel, where I see it daily and it reminds me of a wonderful childhood.

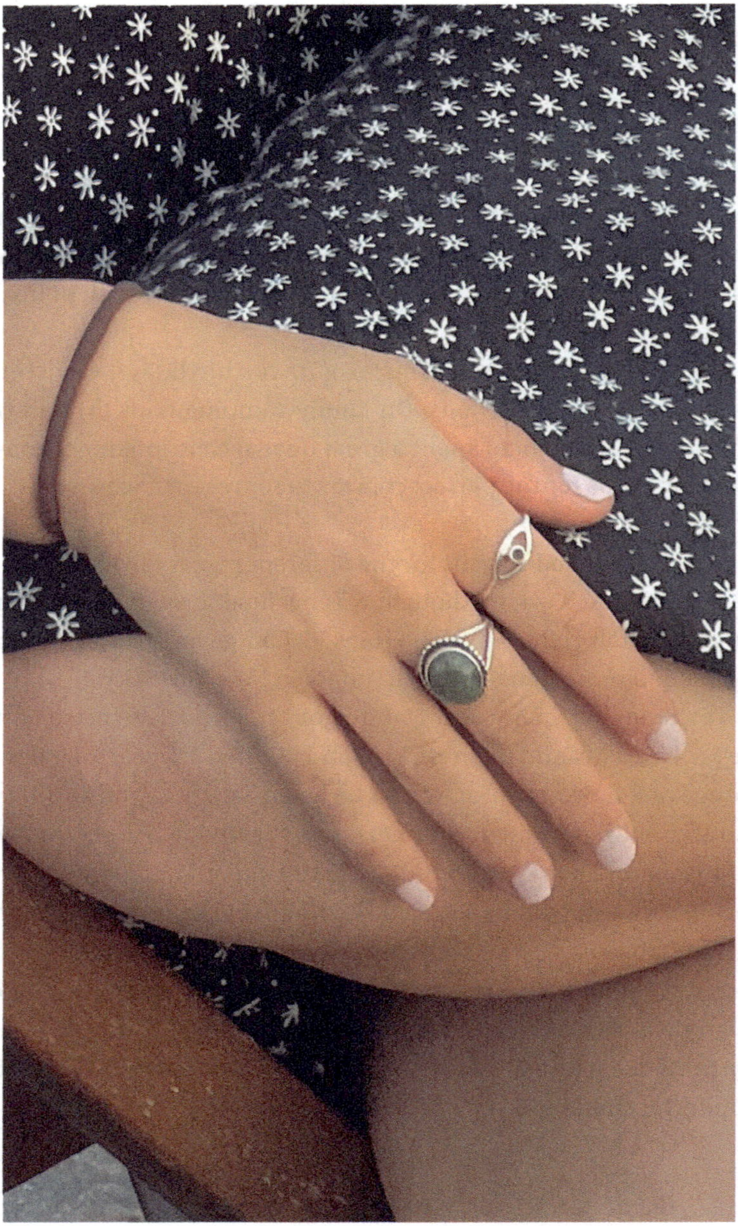

ABIGAIL BROOKS

I'd given her my solemn word. That's how I found myself diving under the murky water, unearthing handful after handful of the ocean's floor, praying that the ring would somehow emerge with the pebbles and grains of sand. My friends laughed at me, ass up in the water, wearing a pair of goggles I'd borrowed from an 8-year-old. I felt like Kim Kardashian searching for her diamond earring. Unlike Kim, the only value this piece held was not monetary, but sentimental.

I'd lost my mom's ring in the ocean. My grandmother had bought it for her on a cherished family vacation when she was a little girl. By most standards, I suppose, the ring looked fairly ordinary: a plain silver band with an olive-green stone in the middle, tarnished from age.

"You can borrow it if you promise never to lose it, my mother had said. "Promise?"

"I promise," I kept repeating.

Whenever my mom saw the ring on my finger, she'd remark how, one day, I might give it to my own child. I'd shrug it off as a silly remark with the same eyeroll whenever she mentioned my future.

Plunging into the water, over and over, I felt this dream my mother envisioned for me being swept away with the tide. No matter how long I combed for that ring, all that kept resurfacing was tremendous guilt. My mother birthed me into this world, endured my temper tantrums, put up with my bratty adolescence, loved me unconditionally, and I repaid her by losing her cherished ring.

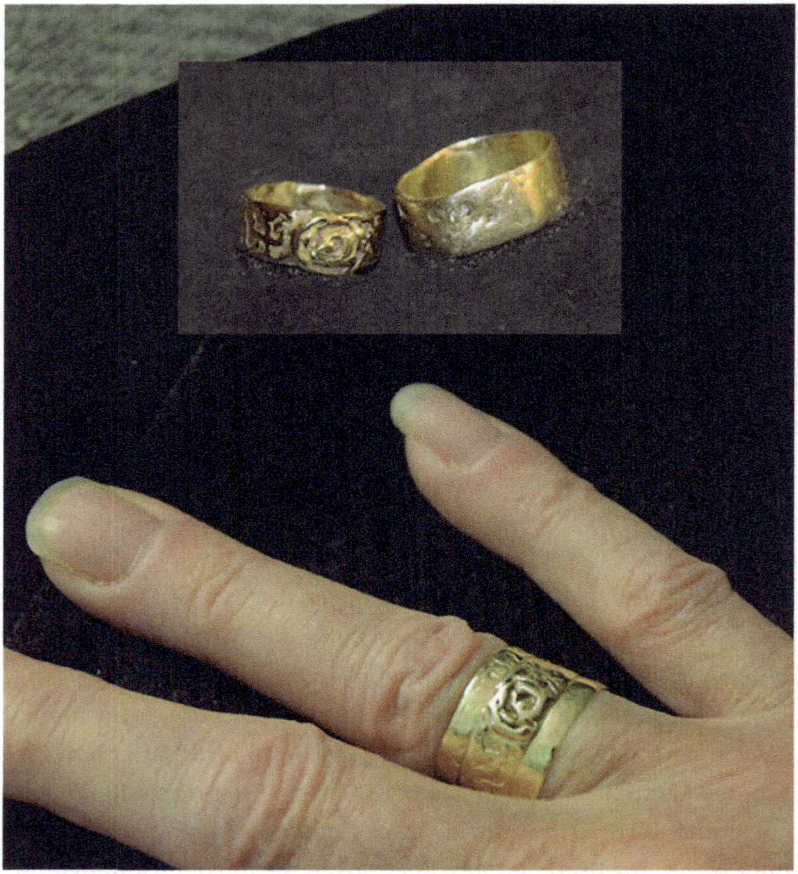

JIM DODDS

As I drive down the hill on Main Street I mutter what I always say when my granddaughter's in the car, from the time she was tiny.

And Maddie still laughs!

It's been eight weeks since my wife Judy's death and the ring is finally ready. I park the car and go in and they show it to me. And I'm just completely blown away.

I've had them take my wedding ring, split it in half and wrap it around hers. And here it is. Big and bold and golden and beautiful and I'm standing there shaking, starting to cry. And it's...just spectacular.

I go out to the car, still shaking, and decide to call my stepdaughter. Eugenie and I spent the last four days with Judy in the nursing home that she always dreaded ending up in.

I took a lock of her hair and I took her wedding ring, after almost 50 years together.

I call Eugenie. She answers and I say, "I just picked up the ring at Perrywinkles."

"I just drove *by* Perrywinkles!"

"Well... come back!"

Waves of grief keep passing over me and I wonder how I'll ever survive.

But I've had an insight that turns the whole process inside out.

That wave *is* her, coming to be with me, and the pain is me not understanding that I'm feeling her touch me. And when the wave comes, I open my heart.

Storied Stuff

BILL DURDEN

The human longing for continuity and the familiar is a powerful drive. For decades my wife and I have traveled to the High Black Forest, Germany (Hinterzarten) for intensive daily hiking.

During our first hike every year, I am on the lookout for a fallen branch that with creative application of my Swiss Army knife can be turned into a sturdy and reliable walking stick. I simply cannot accept the metal walking sticks so ubiquitously available these days, just as I cannot accept metal bats exclusively in use for softball and non-professional baseball. It is wood in firm grip that connects me to my forest path, just as it was in my youth the imprint of the ball on a wooden bat (when I was fortunate enough to strike the ball) that brought me—with sound and feeling—into the game.

At the end of our stay in Germany, I always place that year's iteration of my walking stick along a path so as to be not too visible that I might reclaim it the following year, but visible enough to invite the discerning eye of another hiker to take it up as her own. Upon my return, I look for the stick I left behind. Sometimes I find it and take it up again for another season—nicely weathered during a German winter.

But often I look in my hiding place and the stick is gone. I like to think that it has been recycled—either to another hiker or back to nature from which it came. If that is the case, I begin the delightful search once again for my next generation of wooden walking stick.

Storied Stuff

ROBERT JORDAN

My father started his career in the 1930s, working in the oil fields in Maracaibo, Venezuela. He then enlisted in the Navy in World War II, surviving the invasion of Normandy. After the war we moved to Peru when I was three years old. My experience there shaped much of the rest of my life.

We lived in a tiny seaside oil camp named Talara, north of Lima. My parents collected native pieces during our time there, including three painted drums with animal skin heads. These drums symbolize that period in my life. After returning to the U.S., our dinner table conversation routinely featured tales of Peru, lapsing into Spanish phrases, with commentary about revolutions, oil markets, and daily life in Talara.

My father went on to other international jobs, with a stint in pre-Gaddafi Libya, then Hong Kong, and a later career with USAID including four war-torn years in Vietnam. I pursued my international interests as well, studying French and Russian in college and then in uniform as an officer with the Naval Security Group. My parents passed down the three Peruvian drums to me, and the drums moved with me through decades of travel.

My attraction to international affairs came full circle in 2001 when President George W. Bush asked me to be his ambassador to Saudi Arabia. I took my post a month after the attacks of September 11. After my government service, I later returned to the Middle East to run my law firm's practice in Dubai. Now retired, I view the three drums every day through the lens of my early childhood dreams.

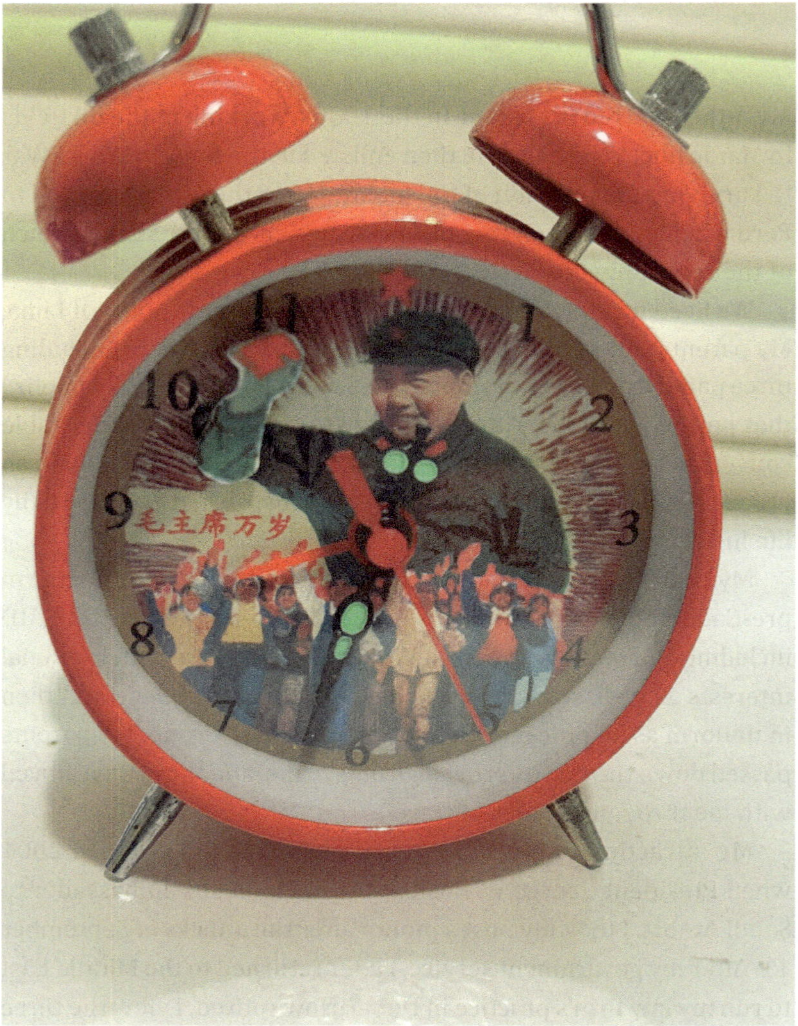
毛主席万岁

MIKE CONKLIN

In the summer of 2009, I taught journalism courses at Xiamen University in China. I was the first participant in an ongoing exchange program between DePaul University, where I was full-time faculty, and the Chinese school.

Xiamen was a beautiful coastal city on the South China Sea with white sand beaches that, like San Francisco, sat on a bay encircling a historical island. In this case, the island, Gulangyu, was a square mile of colorful shops, restaurants, hotels, palatial homes once occupied by wealthy foreigners, and training schools for classical pianists. Motorized vehicles were not permitted on the island.

Xiamen is a modern, domestic tourist destination. The air is clean. Its strip of hotels on the water remind of Miami Beach. The port city also serves as a commercial hub for Southeast Asia. The population then was 4.3 million—7.2 million for the metro area. It easily ranked among the top three or four U.S. cities population-wise. In China, it barely ranks in the top 20.

The university, at 28,000 students, was the size of DePaul. Its neatly laid out campus was lively with benches, gardens, basketball courts, food stands, bike racks, artwork, and spacious buildings. In one corner was a popular art museum with a busy coffee shop. Almost every day I walked through a colorful campus flea market. Nanputuo Temple, a sprawling, serene Buddhist oasis of greenery and meditation stations, was just outside the school's main gate.

Students in my classes were non-stop with questions, mostly wanting to know about American pop culture. They were intrigued by the journalism films I showed in my classrooms. Surely, I am the only person to show "China Syndrome" in China.

This experience demonstrated how little I knew about China. It was a wakeup call. Maybe that's why I purchased this alarm clock in the flea market.

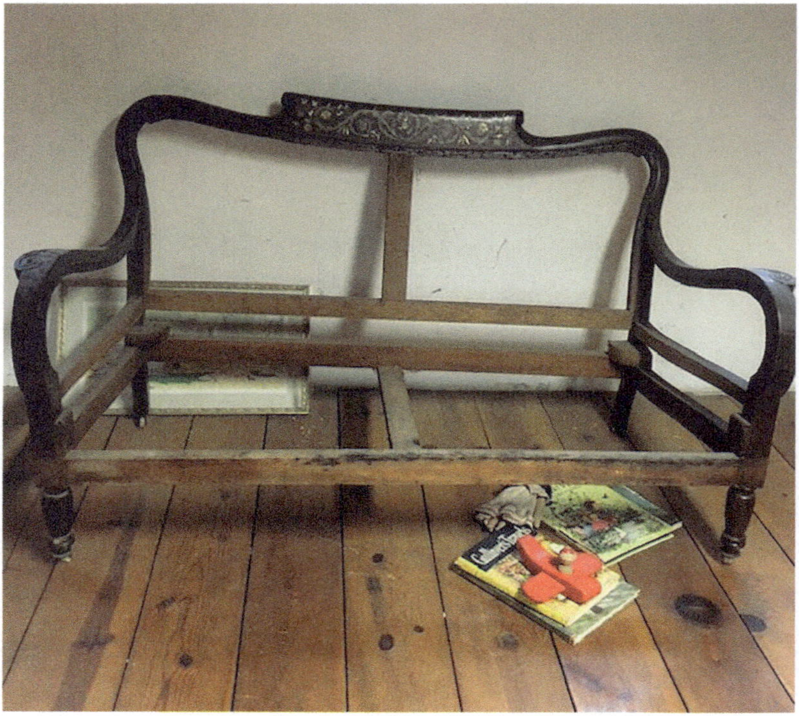

SALLY deVINCENTIS

The yellow house I grew up in had a cellar. Not a basement, but a cellar with a dirt floor, a single light bulb and the damp smell of earth, mold and coal dust. Buried in a corner of this already buried place were the remains of a Victorian love seat. Only her wooden skeleton was left. And there she lay hidden under the cellar steps for forty years... forgotten but not forgotten.

My mother's mother died in the 1918 pandemic. Soon after the funeral my mother was sent away to boarding school. My mother later became a nurse and married my father. Many years later she returned to her childhood home looking for memories of her mother...and in the house's attic she found the bare frame of her mother's Victorian love seat. She took the remains back to her new home with plans to make it beautiful again, but time slipped through my mother's fingers and the bare frame stayed hidden... forgotten but not forgotten.

In 1982 my mother died and the yellow house was sold and emptied, except for the relic in the cellar. I found the sofa there and took her home to my house. For 38 years she has rested in my basement. But in this year of the 2020 pandemic, the sofa is not forgotten. I will make her beautiful again to honor the memories of the mothers she left behind.

Storied Stuff

LARRY COHAN

This month marks the 49th year of our annual gathering of friends to celebrate Chanukah. Over the years we've shared in both joys and sorrows and watched our children grow up and have kids of their own. And it only takes four emails to pin everyone down on a date; the original members aren't exactly pressed for time these days.

As in past years, each youngster will receive a new dreidel, commemorating the occasion. However, this year's celebration will otherwise be quite unusual. Thanks to Covid, like many families we will turn on our respective computers, zoom at the appointed hour, and light our own menorahs together, sorta.

While we're all missing social gatherings and burned out on zoom calls by now, there are a few positives about celebrating Chanukah over the Internet:

We don't have to listen to Millie complain that she doesn't want to be in the same room as Sherman, her ex, and his girlfriend of twenty years. We don't have the tape of Chanukah '87 in electronic format, so we won't be able to see Josie, age 2, unattended and shoveling hors d'ouevres into her face while the adults were too occupied in the next room with Scotches. Josie, now grown up, is employed as a food consultant. Go figure. Also, the kids, stretched in cities across the country, will have little excuse not to attend this year. Lastly, we won't have to eat Chanukah chicken, a 1950s classic involving apricot jam and Catalina salad dressing.

Happy Holidays!

Storied Stuff

BECCA TAYLOR GAY

I have a passion for Christmas decorations, especially anything shiny with vintage appeal, and I have spent much of my adult life treasure-hunting estate sales for those rare finds amongst a sale's jumble of holiday detritus, particularly seeking Shiny Brite ornaments. Often my scrutiny and patience pay off with a true gem, and one by one I have built a collection of favorite vintage baubles.

So please imagine my extreme delight when recently, while cleaning out my deceased uncle's garage, I discovered a large carton marked "Ornaments from Georgie's collection." Georgie Taylor is my paternal grandmother from whom I received my physical features, demeanor, dry skin (and impeccable taste!).

Within this carton was an amazing treasure trove of original Shiny Brite boxes, each containing full sets of ornaments of every description! These had likely remained untouched for decades. After my initial disgruntlement for them having been kept from me all these years, I was simply awe-struck and overwhelmed by the bounty. It felt to me like they had finally come home.

This season, though my grandmother passed 40 years ago, I feel her presence so strongly in my bedroom where I've decorated a table-top tree with some of her treasures. Though I have no actual recollection of her own Christmas trees, I believe they inspired my adult aesthetic and passion for collecting. I sensed such a deep connection to her as I hung each ornament—finer than any I'd ever scavenged—and appreciated each masterpiece as I imagine she must have done when decorating her own tree those many years ago.

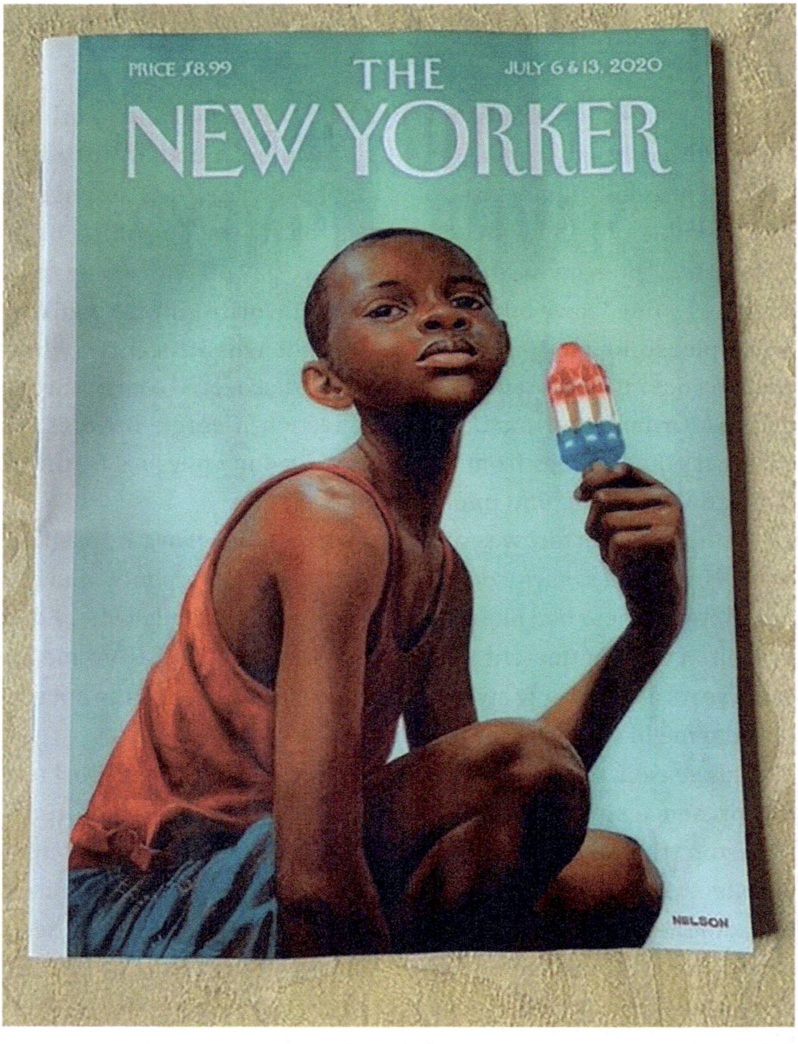
PRICE $8.99
THE
JULY 6 & 13, 2020
NEW YORKER
NELSON

PATRICIA MERRITT LEAR

My dad, Jim Merritt, died young, but wow, what a life. Born the son of a Delaware Indian whose grandfather was the last Chief of the Delaware Nation, some shit must have gone down because my dad was on a tear to get the hell out of Dodge (aka Nowata, Oklahoma) (down by Lightnin' Creek). And whatever us kids were going to be, in his words, "a bunch of half-breeds" was not it.

After bombing all the Germans in the war, my dad started an ice cream factory and manufactured Dreamsicles, Heath Bar Crunches, Eskimo Pies, and all the stuff that will make you fat as a pig. While trying to come up with new designs for ice cream novelty items, one night, he came up with this rocket shape with fins. We kicked around the name, and, given his heroic war exploits, The Bomb Pop was soon unleashed upon the world.

What none of us Merritts saw coming was that beginning in the 2000s, the Bomb Pop would become the iconic Americana symbol of summer. The red, white, and blue Bomb Pop is everywhere. I just saw it today in a Gap ad, and last summer there was a Bomb Pop on the cover of the *New Yorker*.

I don't think any of this just happened. I think my dad is still there, reminding us to reach for the stars, and how better to do that than to put a Bomb Pop in front of our faces when we venture to the Mall, open a flyer from Neiman-Marcus, or even go to Target to buy a float for the beach (in the shape of a Bomb Pop, of course). It's Daddy reaching out, I am sure of it.

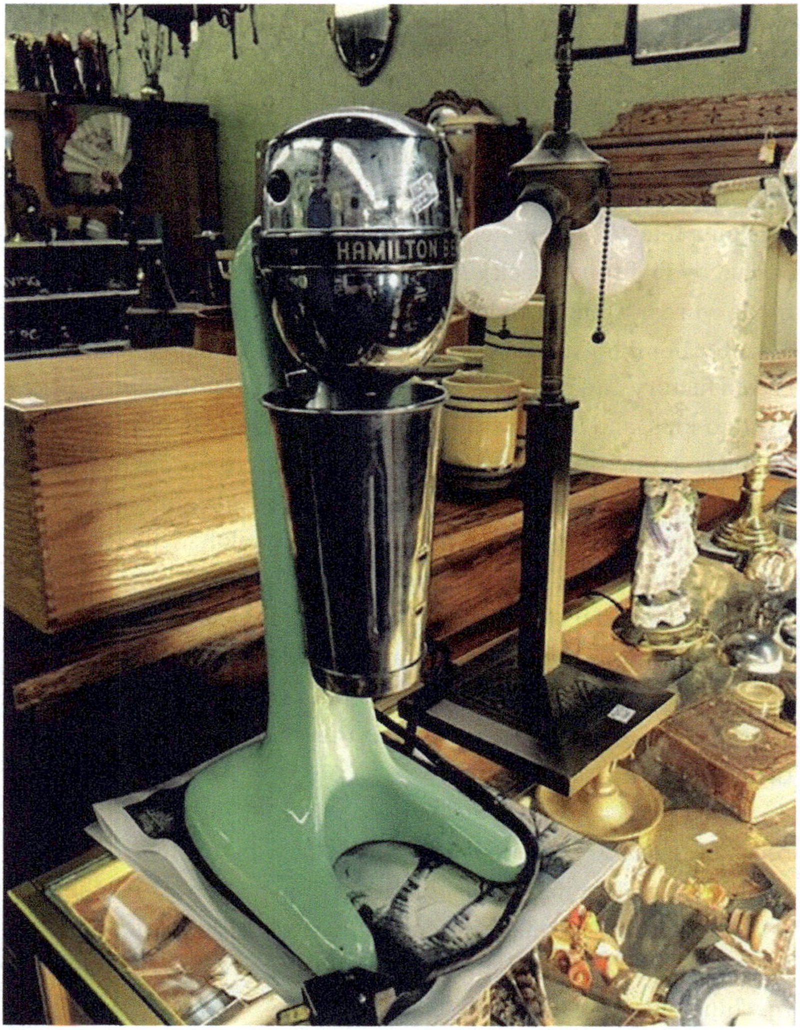
HAMILTON BE

BOBBIE CALHOUN

Whenever my mother, an irascible Brooklynite, would get a hankering for an old-fashioned ice cream soda, made with real seltzer, Hershey's chocolate syrup (no other brand would do), and whipped cream, she pulled this contraption out of the pantry, easily hefting the nearly ten pounds like it was a feather.

The sound of the whirring machine, deafening in our tiny kitchen, brought my three brothers running from all corners of the house, the yard, the garage. Long-haired, bearded, back from college for the summer, they would crowd me out, the little sister, and I knew I wouldn't get the first ice-cold treat that Mom was going to pour from the silvery vessel attached to The Green Monster. We'd run out of tall glasses, too, and I'd get mine in a coffee mug. It didn't matter.

The taste of this confection brought back Brooklyn to my mother. The stories would pour forth like sweet cream, and all of us may as well have been in her old neighborhood, with the shopkeepers out on the sweltering sidewalk, yelling in Yiddish to potential customers to come in, come in, the most delightful things await you inside, *bubbeleh!*

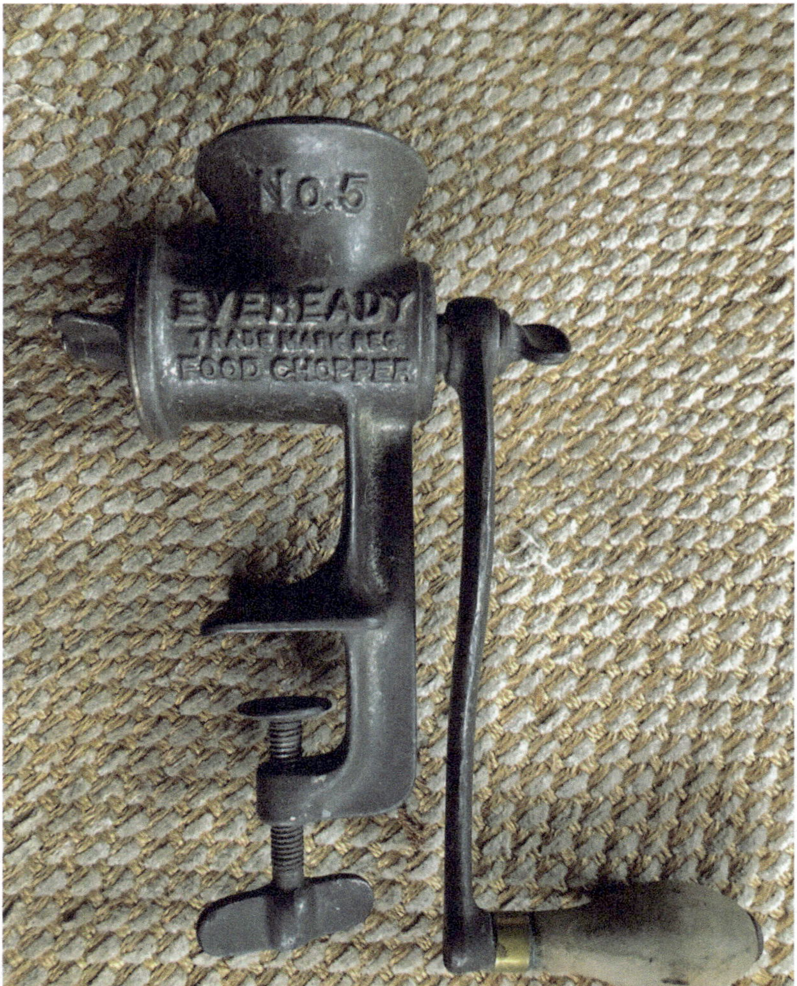
No.5
EVEREADY
TRADE MARK REG.
FOOD CHOPPER

JIM CUNNINGHAM

I remember some of Mom's favorite dinners. She was born one hundred years ago in Pittsburgh to Irish immigrants, and we often ate boiled ham and boiled cabbage and boiled potatoes.

Often a Sunday dinner was a beef chuck roast, cooked a bit too long, with more potatoes, of course. Not always my favorite or most memorable meals, but filling and good eating for a family of seven.

Aah, but the magic happened the next day!

Mom would open the kitchen drawer next to the sink and pull out the battleship-grey No. 5 EVEREADY TRADEMARK REG. FOOD CHOPPER. Clamping it to a kitchen chair, leftover chunks of ham, pickles and other secret ingredients were converted to ham salad and days of glorious sandwiches on white Wonder Bread for school lunches.

Monday after the roast beef dinner, we would be served a delicious hash of beef, potatoes, carrots, and other assorted leftovers.

I remember these leftover dishes more fondly than the original meals. Thanks, Mom!

The meat grinder today looks the same as I remember it years ago. Worn out grey, the feel of metal, worn wooden handle, and yes, I remember washing it and drying it occasionally after it worked its magic.

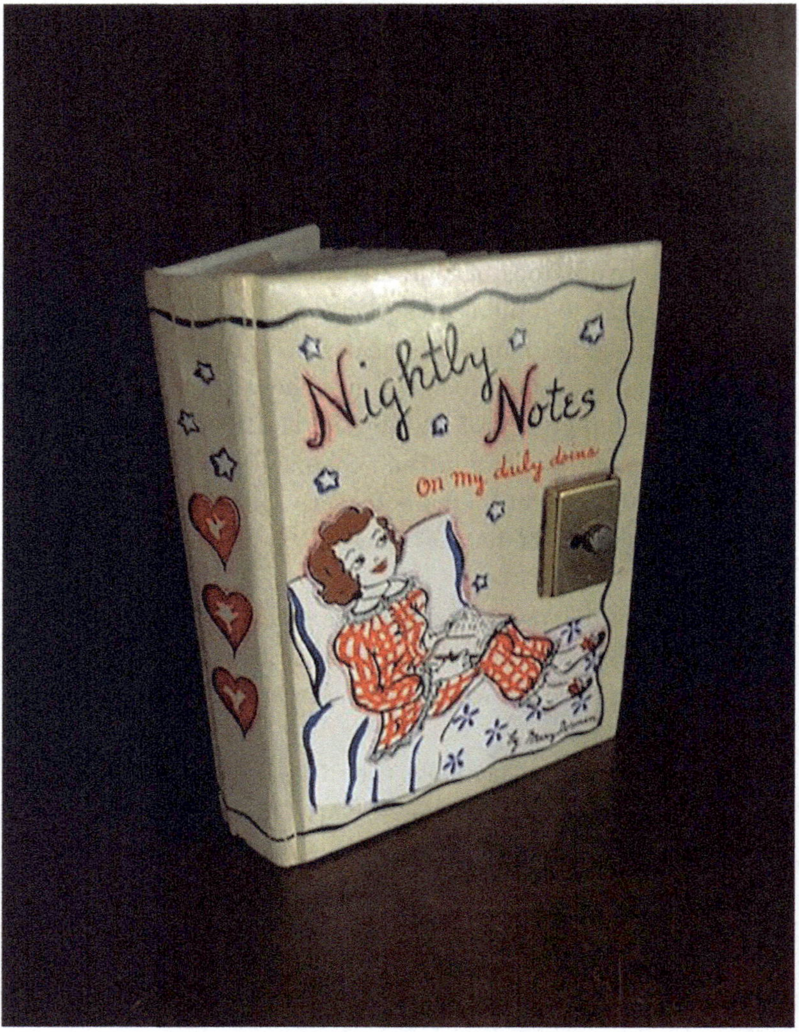
Nightly Notes

PEGGY WAGNER KIMBLE

Do you know what you did every day in 1958? I do. My diary recounts the busy life of eight and nine year old me: bike riding, ice skating, snow forts, the beach, tennis, jumping rope, hula hoops, my doll house, school, piano lessons, dance classes, horseback riding, Brownies, birthday parties, sleepovers, books, movies, day camp, and family trips. Fun with friends, my sister, and my parents. Visits with grandparents, aunts, uncles, and cousins.

I practiced division problems and writing in script. I drew pictures, wrote stories, and invented goofy jokes. I noted my migraine headaches, doctor's appointments, and Iowa Tests. I mentioned that stamps cost 3 cents for postcards and 4 cents for letters. Between the pages I saved a valentine from a boy I liked.

This random year contained momentous events. My baby sister Judy had died two years earlier and I was thrilled when my brother Doug was born in April. In May, our dachshund Fritz bit a boy who had thrown stones at him; when we had to give away our beloved dog, my sister Betsy and I *"were so sad that we could not stop crying."* And in October I proudly wrote, *"I rode on a train to Chicago with no adult."*

Fun, elation, heartbreak, independence: my 1958 diary has them all. Of the many diaries and journals I've written, this is the only one I saved.

I barely recognize her handwriting, but I know that girl. She's been here all along.

Storied Stuff

SUE GANO

Mama was dressed to the nines that day when my class went to the zoo and she came along to herd the first graders from exhibit to exhibit. She put her hair in pink, fluffy curlers the night before and in the morning gleaming waves of chocolate brown appeared as if by magic. She donned a white skirt with pink flowers and stole some shoes from my big sister's closet. "No one needs to know," Mama shared, and I giggled as if I were a party to a crime.

We walked hand in hand, her and I at the end of the two lines my teacher had put us in. We heard lions roar, their sounds cracking in the spring air and watched polar bears dive into their pool to claim their afternoon fish. Our last stop was at the petting zoo, where a goat started to chew on the hem of my Mama's skirt while my classmates laughed.

Upon leaving Mama bought me a key chain in the shape of a bright red elephant. I planned on putting the key to my diary on it and hiding it in my bedside table where I was sure no one would find it.

Fifty-three years later it still resides in my bedside table, albeit a different one, hidden amongst the Kleenex, my writing pad and eyeglasses. The diary key long-gone, the memory of that day spent with Mama as fresh as yesterday.

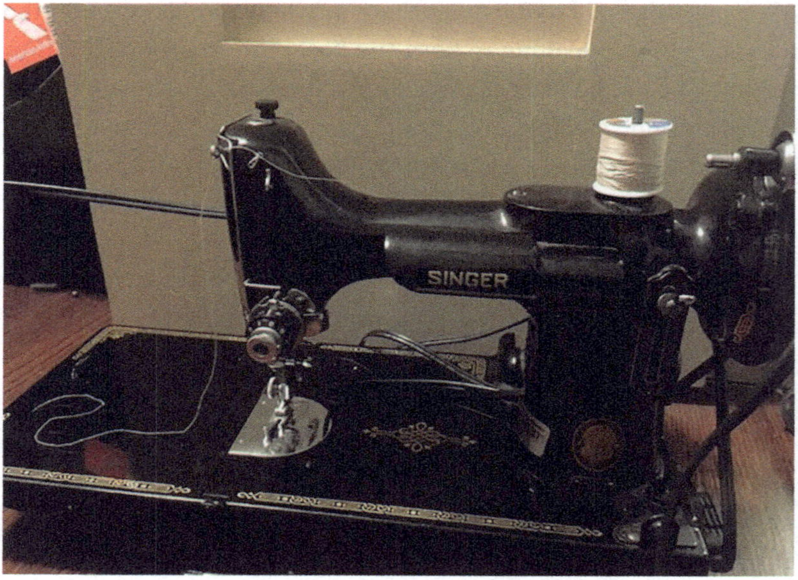
SINGER

CAROL KANTER

Grandma sewed on her Singer with a treadle. I liked to watch her. When I was small, she made some clothes for me and a whole wardrobe for the large, now-antique china doll she gave me, who had been given her and whose eyes opened and shut as she sat up or lay down.

The summer before 8th grade, I wanted to learn to sew. Mom bought me a Singer—electric, with no treadle—and I took a sewing class, learning to use my machine and follow patterns.

When first married, we lived in a six-room student apartment for which I chose different fabrics and whipped up six sets of curtains, no patterns needed. Later, using patterns, I sewed two maternity jumpers for my expanding belly. But these required no proper fit; they just had to be roomy.

Then when our daughters Jodi and Wendy were 5 and 3, my cousin asked if they could be flower girls in her winter wedding. Her bridesmaid gowns would be pink with burgundy trim. I chose a pattern, bought beautiful pink velvet fabric, and burgundy ribbon. I remember feeling very nervous as I made the first cuts in that pristine and rather expensive fabric.

Now whenever I occasionally take out my electric Singer to use for some little project or other, I think of Grandma pumping her treadle and know she'd approve. Because, no matter what, she always approved.

Storied Stuff

PAULA BEARDELL KRIEG

I hadn't crocheted a stitch in years when I enviously watched my friend Susan demonstrate how to create a closure for a folder, using yarn and hook to make something like a scarf that wrapped, like a warm hug, around the folder, keeping it safe and secure.

Did I even have crochet hooks anymore? No. Found a set on-line for six dollars. Carefully punched holes in the edge of a cover that I could now attach yarn to. Picked up my tools, looked at what I had in my hands, willing them to know what to do. My fingers remained still.

How could they have forgotten?

I think about when I was young teenager, flush with cash from my 50 cents an hour babysitting job, walking from my parents' home, downtown to the Five and Dime store. There I bought a book for thirty-five cents, called *the Learn How Book*. My grandmother, who came to this country when she was five, was educated through the sixth grade, was married and pregnant with her first born at age 15, always said that if you can read English, you can learn anything.

With my *Learn How Book* I made things. Crochet was my favorite thing that the book taught. Over the years I made dresses, blankets, scarves, sweaters. My hands were happy with the yarn dancing around the hook in my hand. I could read so I could do everything.

When did I stop? I am no longer young. My own babies are well past their young teenage years. My parent's house was sold, and then sold two times more. I've lived in North Carolina and three different places in New York City. I traveled, too, then settled in rural New York, in a big burnt out shell of an old farmhouse. After thirty years living here, with every square inch of our home lovingly tended to, now full of comfy furniture and bookcases I look at my hands, wondering How To.

My husband sits in his lazy boy, enjoying his morning coffee, our dog napping nearby. I tell my husband about the book I had bought at the 5 and 10 cent store so very long ago. Then I walk into the room that I am sitting in now, pluck that worn and well-loved book off the shelf. Minutes later, my fingers and I are once again dancing with hook and fiber.

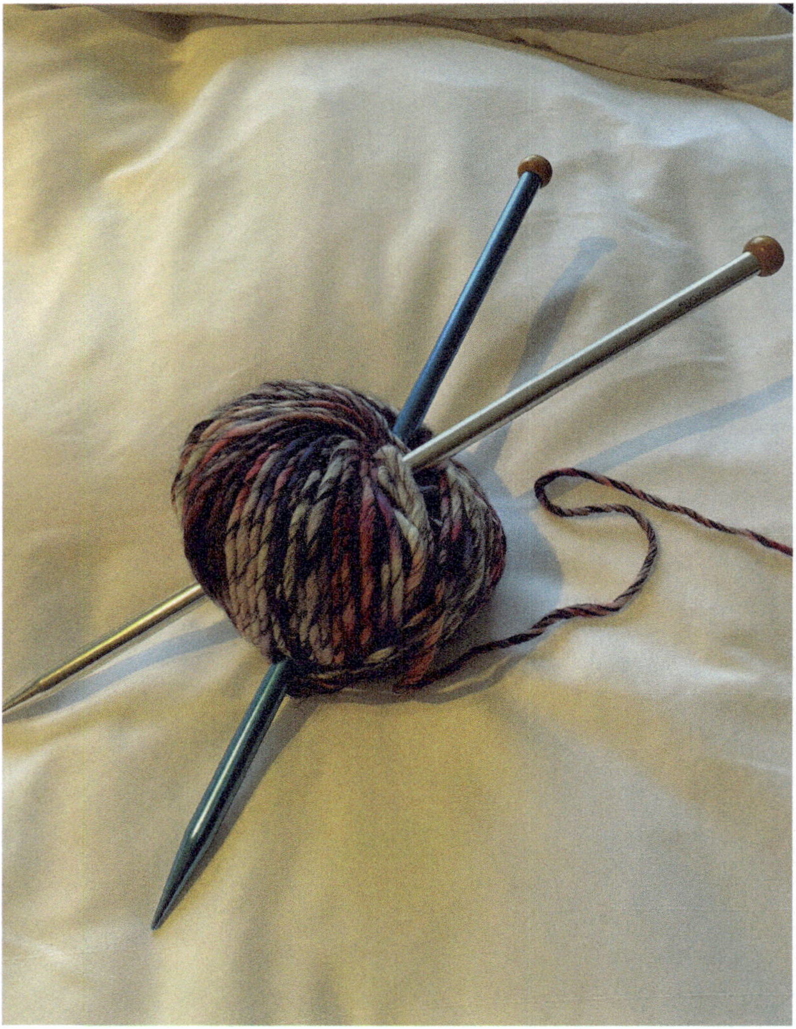

CHRISTINE GOODWIN

My father, a multi-talented man, taught me to knit when I was about 8 years old. I started knitting clothes for my dolls and gradually worked up to larger projects.

During our senior year in high school, my best friend, Marilyn, and I decided we would knit matching cardigan sweaters. We chose a chunky yarn, so the sweaters could be knit in a short time. The thick yarn required size 15 knitting needles. I chose a pair of blue needles and Marilyn chose a pair of silver needles. In a flash of inspiration, we decided to swap one of the needles so we each had one blue needle and one silver needle.

Over the years I have continued to knit and have acquired many pairs of needles of all sizes. Especially since Covid, my knitting projects have multiplied. It's a delight to make a trip to the knit store and choose new skeins from all the beautiful yarns. Every time I start a new project, I take out my collection of knitting needles and those blue and silver No. 15 knitting needles always make me smile!

Storied Stuff

BARBARA HUFFMAN

Some clothing encapsulates a moment, like Jackie Kennedy's pillbox hat or John Travolta's *Saturday Night Fever* white suit. To look at the garment is to remember the moment. For me, my 1970s hip hugger, bell-bottom jeans recall such a certain time.

My fashion, like the 1970s, was experimental and progressive, and I considered myself hot spit in those pants. I owned the jeans in high school and wore them with a fringed suede belt through college. No one else owned anything like them, flared from the knee down, frayed with fabric patches sewn on by hand embroidery covering worn areas. Even looking at the patches evokes memories of the source of the fabric; one patch was made from my homemade purple floral halter top, one was from a dress I sewed in high school, and another was upholstery material from a chair in my parents' living room. Wearing the clothing was wearing those memories, too.

The '70s era and my life at that time were both pivotal. I was leaving home for college, embracing the social movements of the time, and recognizing economic liberties my mother did not know, all changes that encouraged self-expression. Tom Wolfe coined the phrase the "Me" decade to describe the 70s. Those 70s jeans shout "Me", and youth and the freedom and fun of my high school and college years. I've kept those 70s jeans for decades, through multiple moves. Looking at them still makes me smile. I can't fit them on anymore. But they still express me, and who I was when I wore them.

Storied Stuff

MARY CAMPBELL

Stuff. I don't hang on to it. Especially clothes. I regularly perform a cold-blooded ritual of weeding out pieces that I haven't worn in a year. Yet there it hangs almost six decades later—my First Communion dress.

Catholics know First Communion as one in a solemn progression of sacraments or rites through life. For a seven-year-old girl, First Communion is a day when you are the center of attention, have a family party, get some gifts, and act beatified through it all. Plus, you get to wear a fancy white dress and veil.

My mother sewed my dress out of embroidered linen. She worked on it late at night when our house full of kids was finally quiet. With its cotton lining, mother-of-pearl buttons, piped and laced sleeves and collar, the dress is a brilliant piece of craftsmanship. But I didn't like it at the time, preferring to have a store-bought, chiffon dress like many of my classmates. I recall a mild rebuke from my grandma over my less-than-saintly lack of gratitude.

The dress comes out of the closet every now and then. I admire it while alone or sometimes show it off to family or friends. How often do you get to touch a pure act of love?

Storied Stuff

BONNY HOWE

This is my coat from when I was really small (in the mid 1970s). My grandparents had those gas space heaters that you see sometimes in older homes. I liked to stand in front of them to get warm. One time I got too close.

Apparently, my granddaddy acted fast and put it out, which according to my brother made me mad. I may have been a little quick tempered back then.

The coat has been at my mom's house all these years. We recently rediscovered it when getting the house ready to sell. I think she held on to it because it is a part of a story that has often been retold. It's a funny story that could have been tragic.

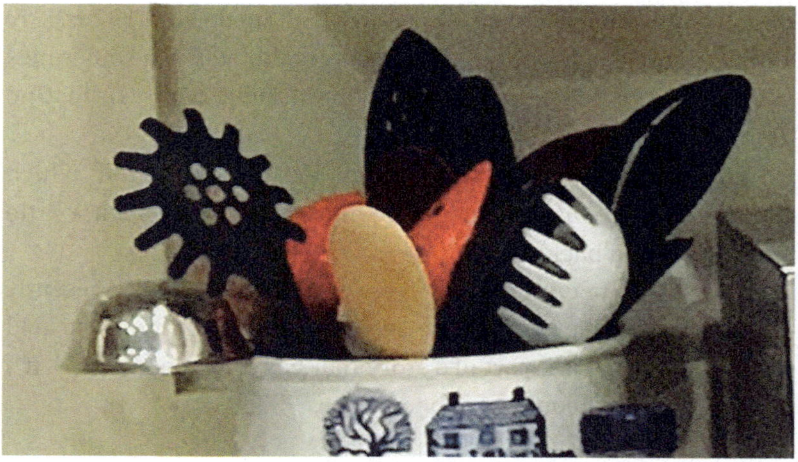

JUDY FRANK FROHLICH

Last November, my husband and I were awakened by an explosion. By the time we got to the living room, it was on fire. Within moments, dense gray smoke filled the room and water poured from the ceiling sprinklers. I couldn't see my husband, but I heard him yell, "Get out!"

Because of a defective lithium battery, we were out of our home for eight months, living in a furnished apartment while our condo was being taken apart and put back together. We had very little control over what was done; all our possessions were taken out of our home and either thrown away or cleaned and stored by strangers.

We ordered replacements for the items we knew had been destroyed, but it wasn't until we finally moved back home that we discovered losses we didn't know we'd had – the small things you don't remember until you need them.

A few days ago, when boiling eggs, I reached for my favorite red plastic cooking spoon and realized it wasn't in the canister on the counter. The spoon had been my mother's; it probably cost her less than a dollar. Mom died seventeen years ago and when I'd use that spoon, I'd often picture her stirring ketchup and grape jelly while making sweet and sour meatballs. But it was gone now, and a profound sense of sadness washed over me. I stood alone and adrift in my newly restored kitchen; it was the first time I cried since the fire.

Storied Stuff

KAREN FULKS

Here's what I remember: every year we went to the Illinois County Fair (in Peoria), mainly because it was blocks from our house and we could hear it, we could see it and we could definitely smell it.

One of the first times I remember clearly was when I was probably nine. My mom took all four of us kids, and we were walking through the exhibition halls. Most of it was farming related, but then we turned a corner and what we saw we couldn't believe. There were two "things" on the table, and there was a mechanical sound coming from one. As the woman behind the table started explaining what this was, I vaguely remember my mom trying to get us away, but to no avail.

We were to witness the effects of cigarette smoking on the lungs (sponsored by the American Lung Association), the HORRIBLE effects of cigarette smoking. My mom smoked. All four of us stood mesmerized as the woman went on and on and then, as if something had hit all of us, we started crying. Sobbing. Wailing, *I don't want you to die, please don't sm*oke, *Mommmmmmmmm*.....

Mom quickly ushered us down the aisle and around the corner. There was the printer's union booth, handing out pieces of type. A kind man handed one over to me and said, "The Lord's Prayer is at the end of this, can you read it?" I could, and I was amazed.

That was 64 years ago. I have lost furniture and friends, but for whatever reason, I still have this 7/8" type slug, although, I cannot read it anymore...even with a magnifying glass.

Storied Stuff

REED IDE

The early 18th century barn still stands, still bereft of all indoor stalls, with only a haymow on two sides, just as it was in the 1960s. Today, the only difference is a low red addition to the left side. The outside of the main section looks the same with weatherbeaten siding clinging to its timber frame. It still has its smaller, human-sized doorway, through which we entered the cavernous interior most mornings. To this day it *and* Maggie Tourtellotte remain in my memory as a poignant day I shall hold dear forever.

    Located just off the main drag and down a short hill from the town's school, the barn was perfect for freshmen just learning to smoke. Eight young teenagers "practiced" each morning before school began – until the secretary to Headmaster Alan Walker interrupted my Geometry class one afternoon to hand me an envelope with my name on the front. Unknown to me, seven other students had their classes similarly interrupted. Being a sophomore, I was especially vulnerable to notes that had to be sent home. Nothing that day required my parents' signature – thank God. Inside my envelope was an invitation from Maggie Tourtellotte for breakfast the following morning.

    Maggie, in my youthful eyes, was the epitome of what a proper country Lady should be. With her short cut dark hair and her private school teacher's demeanor, she was every inch the stalwart town scion I needed her to be.

    My mother had Mrs. Conkey from our church, who was constantly held up to my younger brother and me as the epitome of manners at the dinner table. But I had Maggie Tourtellotte, author of early nineteenth century tales of our country town *and* head of the Theft Detecting Society, which our citizens held dear.

It was with no small amount of trepidation that I joined my compatriots outside her home the following morning. Quaking, six boys and two girls (Yes, we boys liked allowing girls into our midst at that point in our pubescent lives.) rang her doorbell promptly at 7:30 in the morning. We all agreed that we should hide our cigarette packs until we knew more about what might be on the other side of that front door.

Our collected fears were unfounded. Maggie turned out to be a wonderful hostess. Ashtrays were placed strategically in her well-appointed, even luxurious, living room. Coffee (with milk, cream and sugar), juice, and a wide assortment of Danish and French pastries were in abundance. Everyone quickly lit up, even Maggie. I was suitably shocked.

Another revelation came. Maggie owned "our" barn. Following social amenities, she offered a worthy compromise, precluding the barn's burning to the ground some morning in the future. She said her patio, outside of her kitchen, was ideal for cigarette smoking. She would provide ashtrays, even juice if she had it some mornings. We could smoke there all we wanted.

This was a handsome offer in 1962. We all agreed at once, smoking again.

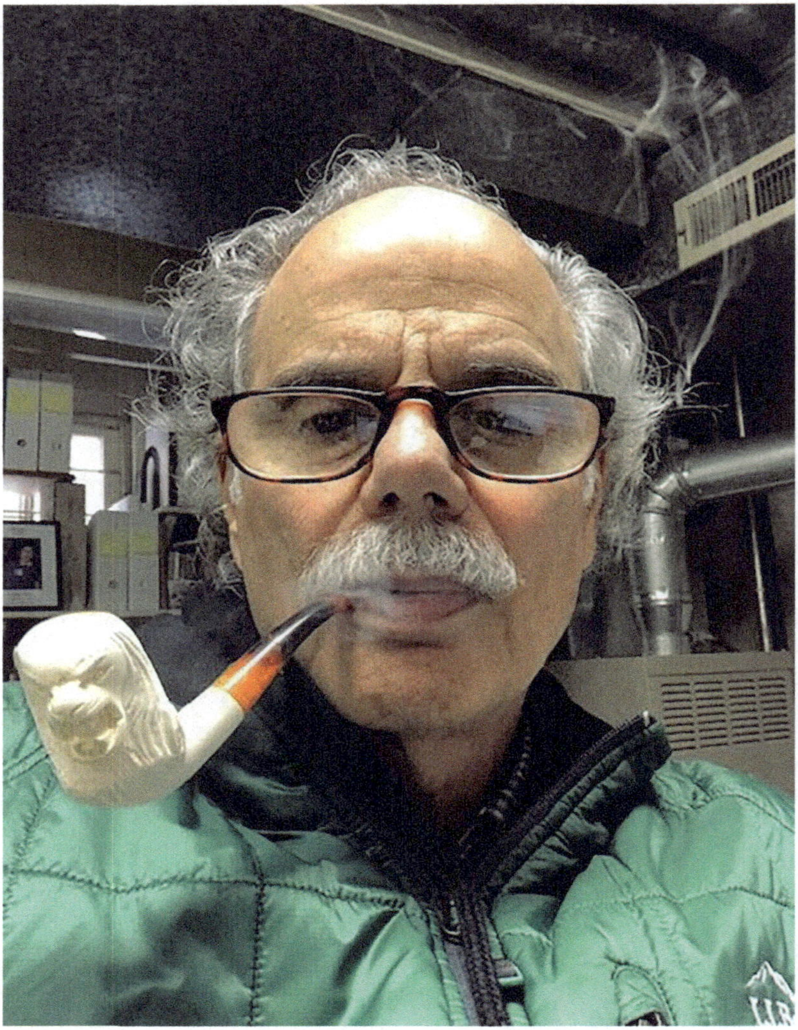

LESTER JACOBSON

Lately I've taken up smoking a pipe. It's a comforting habit, sitting at one's keyboard gripping a pipe stem with satisfying resolve and expelling great clouds of white smoke like the Vatican announcing the new pope. It's also a trifle ridiculous, since no one smokes a pipe anymore. It's gone out of fashion.

That wasn't the case when I took up the habit in college. Over the years I built up a decent collection, including a wonderful meerschaum, the sovereign of pipes. Meerschaums are made from soft white clay and maintain a cool, refreshing smoke right down to the bottom of the bowl. They darken as they age, acquiring a handsome golden patina. Aside from the meerschaum I had perhaps eight or nine other pipes, all attractive and "good smokers."

But then I stopped. I don't remember when or why. My collection disappeared too. Did I sell it? Give it away? Unlikely, I'm a hoarder by nature.

When I resumed pipe smoking a couple of years ago, I had to start a new collection. But somewhere around the house, I suspected, the old pipes were still squirreled away, just awaiting discovery. I even dreamt about them. In the dream I opened a door to an obscure closet and discovered a dresser stuffed with long-lost items: gloves, socks, hats. Stashed among them, I was sure, were the pipes!

Alas, there was no forgotten closet (I've looked). Still, I keep hoping to stumble into the Dresser of Lost Items. I know it's around here somewhere!

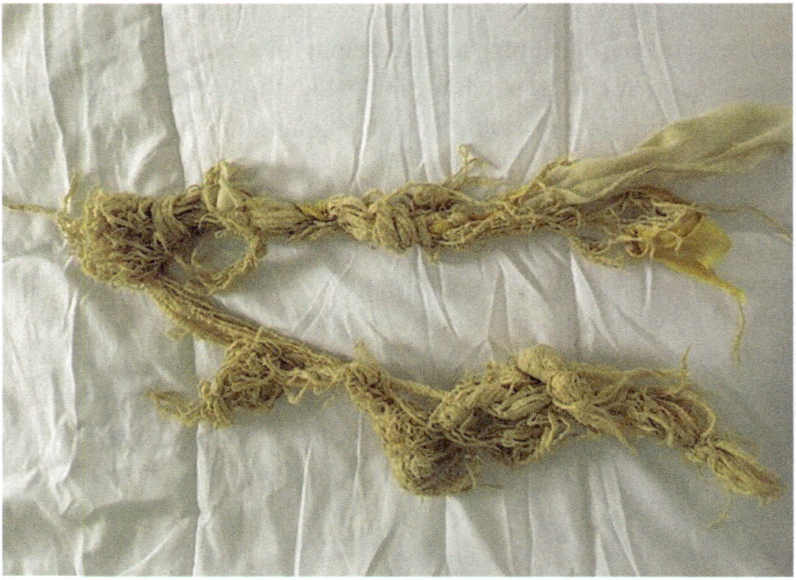

MELISSA HUNT

It used to be a quilt. 5'x7' with beautiful squares of fabric in reds, yellows, oranges, and golds. My great grandmother made it for me when I was born. I don't have a memory without it. Our existence, my blanket and mine, happened simultaneously.

An inanimate object was my first champion. True, it couldn't give me praises or tell me everything was going to be ok, but it didn't need to. It could hug me tightly if I wrapped it around my body. It kept me warm when I was cold. It made hard surfaces soft. It gave me courage when I felt scared. It dried my tears when I was sad.

As happens in life, time got to my blanket. The gorgeous quilt slowly became smaller and smaller with every wash. The fabric frayed and disintegrated until all that was left were strings and fibers tied together in knots to keep it in one piece. What looked like a rag to some remained a prized possession to me.

For years well after childhood, I kept it hidden away from judgment as I went through life's ups and downs, but it was always there. Even after I got married, it stayed under my pillow for me to hold when adulthood overwhelmed.

I'm now 43, and my blanket rests in my dresser in a kind of stasis. When I come across it and run my fingers over its knots, its power to calm and soothe is immediately restored. A champion-in-waiting still.

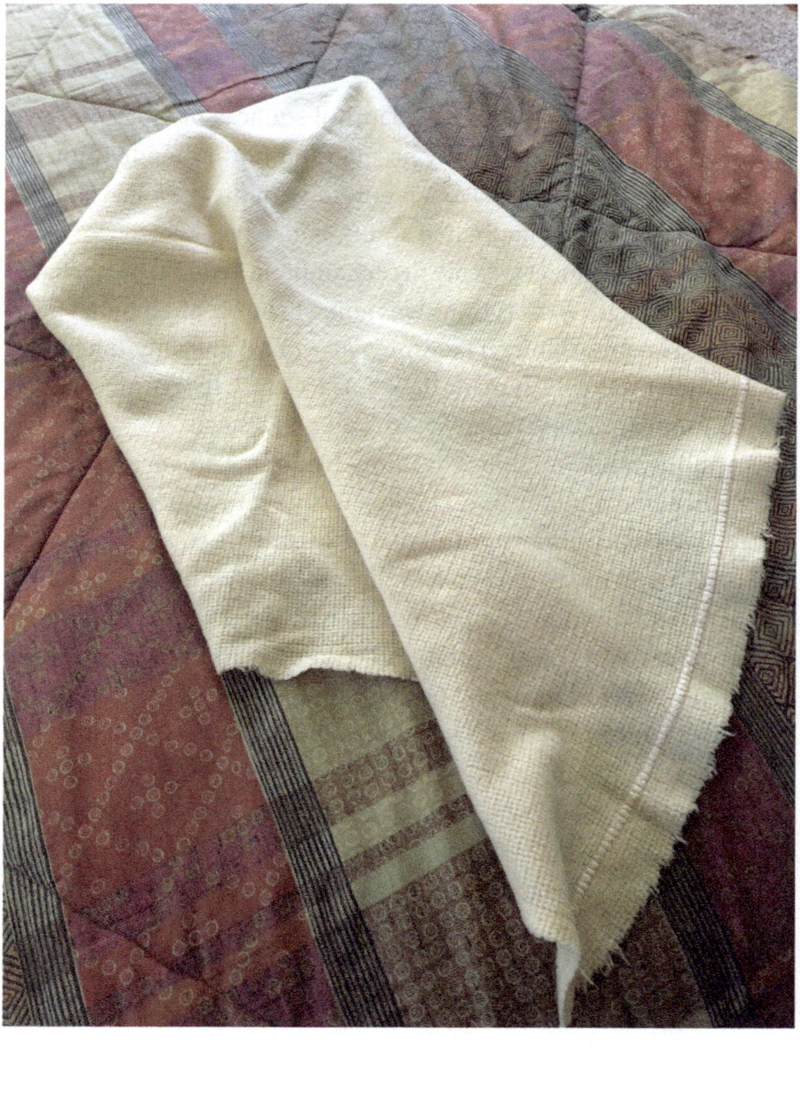

JEAN DIAMOND

He hasn't seen the light of day for years, but I knew exactly where he was: at the bottom of a stack of out of season clothes in the headboard storage of my bed. He isn't soft or pretty. According to his tag, he is 100% virgin wool. My mom told me that he was originally pink, but to me he has always been a faded, yellowish tan. At 63 years old, he is still in pretty good shape, no holes, no fraying. During his first years, he worked a lot—wrapped around me at night and my dolls (and the dog) during the day.

    I don't think I took him to college, and I don't remember packing him up when I left home for good. But here he is, so I must have. He wasn't used when my boys were babies; for one thing he didn't seem soft enough to cradle them and, more importantly, he was mine.

    When I was three, I was seriously ill with an infection behind my eye. My main memory is of my Nana walking me down the hall to surgery, holding Binky and promising that they would be waiting for me. Not too long after that, my mom gave me the choice of giving up my pacifier or Binky. I was old enough to reason that I'd have to give up the pacifier at some point, but I could always keep Binky. And I will.

Storied Stuff

DAVID INLANDER

When I was nine, I suffered from extreme shyness. Lining up in gym class by height, I was always second to last. Thank goodness for Dickie Yee who flanked me to the left.

In an effort to boost my self-confidence, my 6' father dragged me to register for boxing classes at the Highland Park Recreational Center. My grizzled coach, Police Chief Michael Bonamarte, was determined to shape a bunch of timid little boys into the next Floyd Patterson! For the next eight weeks, I ran laps, jumped rope, shadow boxed, and eventually sparred with the imposing Chief himself. Little by little, my fears subsided, and I keenly focused on keeping my left hand up to protect my nose from the next incoming jab.

The Chief announced an elimination tournament would determine each grade's champion. I fought three matches, advancing to the finals against HUGE Gordon Sheppi, who tipped the scales 42 pounds more than I. Either out of fear or cunning, I danced around the ring and wore Gordon down—so by the final round, I landed several decisive punches to my panting, red-faced opponent.

Victory was mine, and I proudly accepted my "Golden Gloves" trophy! Despite my diminutive size, I realized I could hold my own and overcome imposing obstacles. Over time, shyness and shortness fell by the wayside. My confidence grew, inspired by the proudly displayed hardware on my bookshelf, which now resides next to my only other athletic award: 2019 Fantasy Football League Champion!

Storied Stuff

KEN HERSH

Peace.

When my friend Dave put a fly rod into his hand, it became a natural extension of his arm.

When my friend Dave stepped knee deep into a mountain stream, he became a natural structure in the river for the water to part as it rolled past his stance.

When my friend Dave cast a dry fly onto the river ahead of the waiting fish, he lost himself in the moment.

When my friend Dave was fly fishing, he had no cancer. He only had the now. He had peace.

I was honored that Dave spent one of his last moments of clarity with me at my retreat on New Mexico's Pecos River battling wits with finicky trout. Time stood still on that crisp fall September day in 2015.

Watching a man who had weeks or months to live find joy in that battle was a lesson I was blessed to have him teach: Don't be afraid to lose yourself. Find your joy. Find your peace.

Now, I find that on "Dave's Run."

Love and miss you, Dave.

Storied Stuff

LINDA GARTZ

After my mom's death from peritoneal cancer in 1994, my brothers and I scoured our former home, separating trash from treasure. In the attic we discovered a trove of family history: World War II letters, letters between my parents, family passports, postcards, diaries, diplomas, scores of photos, and nearly 100 letters from the old country (today, Romania).

As we searched further, we found both my parents' diaries, Mom's starting in 1927 and spanning almost sixty years. Dad also kept diaries, first as a young man and again as a young father, far from home. For thirteen years, he and Mom wrote letters to each other, sharing their loneliness, work, and Mom's stress, running our sprawling rooming house.

Mom had typed and saved detailed notes for psychiatrists about her mentally ill mother and the heartache and chaos Grandma K created in our home, during the fifteen years she lived with us.

We separated our finds into twenty-five bankers' boxes and stored them in my garage. When I finally started reading, I was hooked. Whisked back in time across decades, I was determined to write a book, searching for and eventually finding focus in the heinous redlining policies that had segregated our West Side community, the rapid racial change Mom had documented, and their thirty years as landlords as our beloved neighborhood was devastated by two riots.

I realized that if I didn't find a home for these treasures, this unique first-person history would be lost forever. In 2010, I emailed the Newberry Library's Midwest Manuscripts Collection. Director Martha Briggs responded immediately to set up a meeting.

I watched her page through some sample diaries and the detailed spreadsheets my brothers and I had created of the archive contents. She looked up and said, "We want it all."

I was thrilled! This venerable Chicago research library would house the Gartz Family papers along with those of famous luminaries like columnist, Mike Royko. I kept the archives at home to continue research for my book, over time, adding my own papers and photos.

Finally, on May 24, 2021, I made the transfer official, filling a van with the boxes and delivering them to Alison Hinderliter, the new director of the Newberry's Midwest Manuscripts.

It's been an incredible journey from first discovery to donation. I can rest easy, knowing that this vast trove of our family's history will contribute to scholarship and research for decades, hopefully centuries, to come. It pays to keep such storied stuff.

Storied Stuff

SHARON FIFFER

1995. College shopping with daughter, Kate. Extra-long sheets, pillows, comforter, a blanket with the sun and moon on it, towels, cute plastic containers for toiletries, toiletries, a poster or two, notebooks, pens, a boxy Mac computer. Several trips to local Bed, Bath and Beyond resulting in shopping bags filled to overflowing. All stuffed into car.

2002. College shopping with daughter, Nora. Extra-long sheets, laptop. The day before move-in, one trip to Bed, Bath and Beyond in NYC resulting in several shopping bags filled to overflowing stuffed in a taxi.

2006. College shopping with son, Rob. Extra-long sheets. Trip to Bed, Bath and Beyond cut short when he commandeered shopping cart and insisted, "I don't need any of this stuff."

In 1969, did I go college shopping with my mother, Nellie? Nope. She didn't approve of my heading off to The University of Illinois. I heard her ask my dad, "Why is she going? What does she need college for anyway?"

My relationship with Nellie was complicated. I never doubted that she loved me fiercely, but I was certain she had no idea who I was. It's taken me a lifetime to realize I didn't know her any better.

Walking through a gift shop, I pointed to a ceramic ashtray.

"Will you buy me that?" I asked. It wasn't cheap. And the EZ Way Inn, my parents' tavern, had dozens of ashtrays, mine for the taking.

"What for? You don't smoke."

"But I'm going to college next month. I'll have friends who smoke."

Nellie bought me the ashtray.

In my room, 914 Illini Tower, I placed the ashtray on my desk. I loved looking at it. I also started smoking.

It's now been over 40 years since I had a cigarette. The ashtray remains on my desk. I still love looking at it. And remembering that Nellie bought it for me, for college, even though I didn't smoke. And even though she didn't want me to leave.

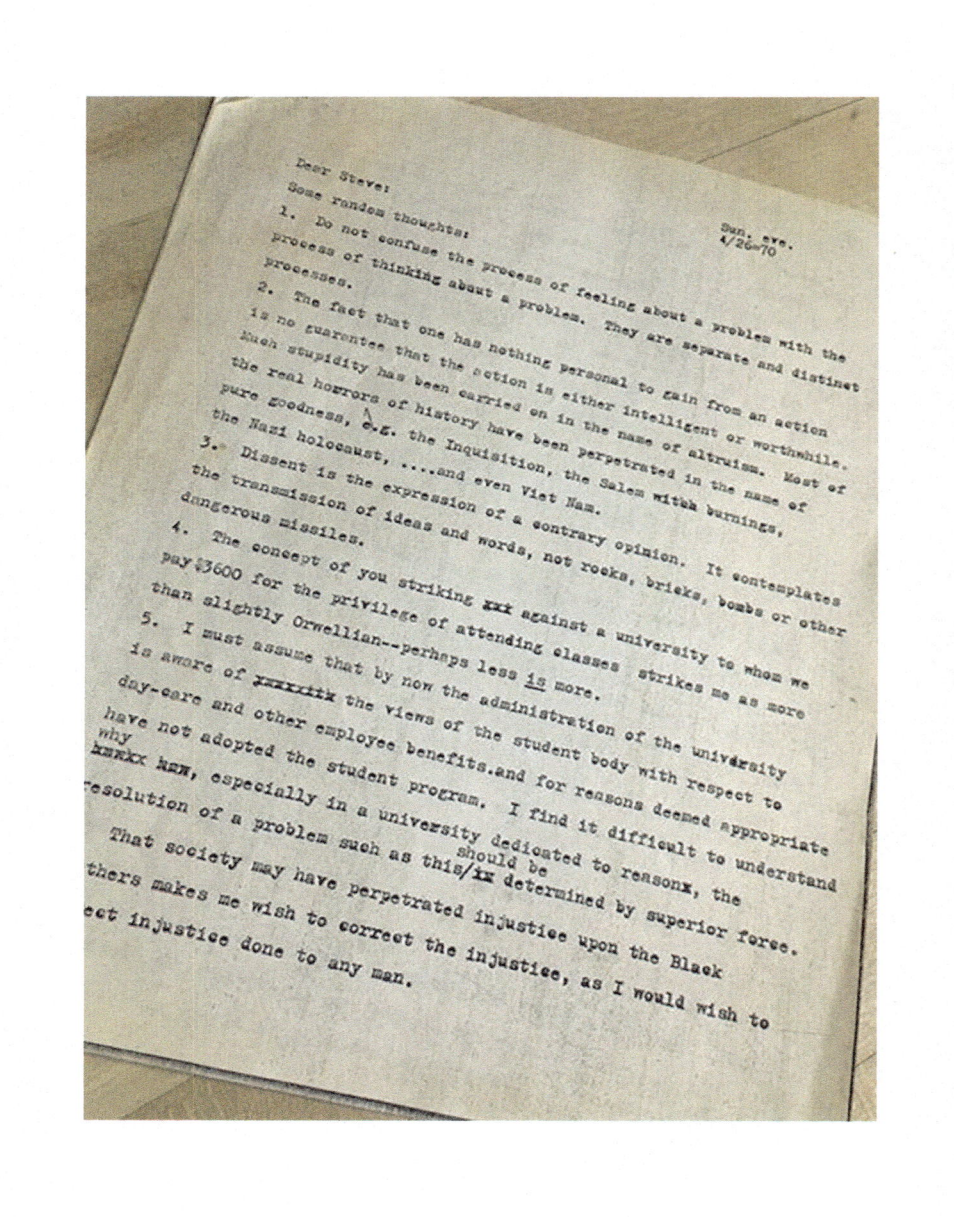

Dear Steve:
Some random thoughts:

Sun. eve.
4/26-70

1. Do not confuse the process of feeling about a problem with the process of thinking about a problem. They are separate and distinct processes.

2. The fact that one has nothing personal to gain from an action is no guarantee that the action is either intelligent or worthwhile. Much stupidity has been carried on in the name of altruism. Most of the real horrors of history have been perpetrated in the name of pure goodness, e.g. the Inquisition, the Salem witch burnings, the Nazi holocaust, ...and even Viet Nam.

3. Dissent is the expression of a contrary opinion. It contemplates the transmission of ideas and words, not rocks, bricks, bombs or other dangerous missiles.

4. The concept of you striking out against a university to whom we pay $3600 for the privilege of attending classes strikes me as more than slightly Orwellian--perhaps less is more.

5. I must assume that by now the administration of the university is aware of the views of the student body with respect to day-care and other employee benefits.and for reasons deemed appropriate have not adopted the student program. I find it difficult to understand why, especially in a university dedicated to reason, the resolution of a problem such as this/ should be determined by superior force. That society may have perpetrated injustice upon the Black others makes me wish to correct the injustice, as I would wish to correct injustice done to any man.

STEVE FIFFER

At age nine in 1959, I sent my hero, the NY Yankees' Mickey Mantle, a letter inviting him to dinner. The following year, I sent a letter to another hero—John F. Kennedy—wishing him success in his race for president. Framed and under glass, their personalized, autographed responses still grace my office wall. But it is another letter—this one unsolicited—that I cherish most.

When I was a sophomore at Yale in the spring of 1970, I joined the vast majority of my fellow students in a strike protesting the arrest of the Black Panther leader Bobby Seale, President Nixon's bombing of Cambodia, and the university's treatment of its blue collar workers. The strike, which preceded May Day protests across the country, received national attention. And I received a letter from my lawyer-father, a liberal Democrat, with what he termed "Some random thoughts."

His ten numbered paragraphs were hardly random. Number One cautioned me not to "confuse the process of feeling about a problem with the process of thinking about a problem." In Number Four, he said he found "the idea of striking against a university to whom we pay $3600 for the privilege of attending classes" (yes $3600!) "slightly Orwellian." He was no fan of the Panthers, but in Number Six, he said that it was incumbent on society to "correct the injustice (done them)."

There are nuggets of wisdom in all ten paragraphs, but it is the final one that still brings a tear to my eye. I picture him in his study pecking away on his old Royal typewriter—thoughtfully tempering his own philosophy with the right of his oldest son to grow up and even make mistakes. It reads:

"I am pleased with your sensitivity to injustice...unhappy that you will miss some excellent classes, envious of the exhilaration of an all-consuming cause (I've known it), slightly concerned for your physical well-being, and confident that you will survive your days on the barricade as I survived mine."
   Much love,
   Dad

Contributor Biographies

Gabi Coatsworth is an award-winning British-born author and blogger, who has spent half her life living in the United States. Her memoir, *Love's Journey Home*, was published by Atmosphere Press in May 2022 and a prequel about her British childhood is due in 2026. https://linktr.ee/gabicoatsworth

Adrienne Gallagher is a former interior designer whose career focused mainly on the project management and interior design of corporate headquarters and law firm offices. She and her husband, Barney, managed to raise their three children—in Winnetka, Illinois; Portola Valley, California; Basel, Switzerland; and Glencoe, Illinois—without resorting to *Robert's Rules of Order*.

Esther Cohen posts a poem every day on Substack at Overheard. She lives in New York City. Esthercohen.com.

Jim Dorr is a happily retired lawyer - an avid fly fisherman, collector of old tackle and occasional writer.

Beth Inlander is a retired banker, mother and grandmother who loves to read, take classes and partake in lively discussions in book and movie groups. Beth serves on multiple philanthropic boards and can often be found out to dinner, at plays and listening to music with her husband around Chicago.

Arnie Kanter writes: "At 82, I can't do a 2-sentence bio, so this one sentence will have to do." www.innovation80.org

Evalynne Gould Elias is a Jersey girl, Manhattanite, San Francisco resident who somehow ended up living in Lexington, KY, for the last 35 years. Working on retiring from her private psychotherapy practice, any day now, she has a great husband, two great kids, and two unbelievably fabulous grandchildren.

Francie Arenson Dickman is an essayist, college essay coach and author of the novel, Chuckerman Makes a Movie. To learn more, visit her website https://franciearensondickman.com.

Jack Hertz is a lawyer practicing in Northbrook, IL. He is a proud native son of Pittsburgh and grandfather of twelve.

Jack Doppelt is an emeritus journalism prof who's created a music lyrics game with his son.

Junior Burke is a songwriter and novelist. He lives Out West.

Noelle Allen is the mother of two adult, feminist children and is also the caretaker of 4 cats and a turtle. She teaches high school language arts and lives in Portland, Oregon.

Laura B. Becker, a retired academic speech-language pathologist, is now a volunteer Gallery Guide at the Museum of Fine Arts Boston and a Study Group Member and Leader at the Harvard Institute for Learning in Retirement.

Nancy O'Brien Dorr is a retired grandmother to seven.

Phil Kirschbaum launched his life as a writer in 2018 after retiring from a forty-year career as a psychotherapist and organizational consultant.

Judith Kassouf Cummings writes from her outpost in northern Illinois where she teaches students of all ages online. She is a member of the Illinois State Poets Society, (ISPS) the Rockford Writers' Guild, Poets & Patrons, and Poets for Peace.

Contributor Biographies

Carol Bobrow was a professional dancer for forty years and is currently an amateur painter and a volunteer for a food pantry.

James Finn Garner is the author of the Politically Correct Bedtime Stories series and the Rex Koko, Private Clown series. His eponymous website is named after him: www.jamesfinngarner.com

Cathy Kinard is a Critical Care nurse for 49 years who now continues to work as a full-time home infusion nurse....which was supposed to be her retirement job.....and never meant to be full-time.

Kathryn L Kaplan, PhD, a Glencoe, Illinois, native now living abroad, has a grief support private practice, *Heartfelt Spaces*, and is the author of *Becoming Visible to Myself: An Unexpected Memoir* and *Dying With His Eyes Wide Open: A Memoir of Love and Grief*.

Judi Geake facilitates several memoir groups, encouraging everyone she comes in contact with to get their stories on paper. She, herself, has over 300 entries in her Memoir Book.

Joe Garber is a retired former actor, stage manager, producer, children's theatre playwright, director and Senior Business Representative for Actor's Equity Association. Other than playing pickleball and traveling, he is still figuring out what should come next in his life.

Larry Gritton, Central School '64 Best Class Ever, is a retired lawyer. He now spends almost half the time in Arizona playing a lot of poker and making new friends and enjoying the Arizona winters.

Susie Butterfield is a lifelong antiquer and junker, growing up in a family of carpenters and artists who enjoyed a unique sense of humor.

Julie Cowan is a multi-disciplinary artist based in Evanston, IL. She is director of artruck, a community art project founded in 2011 as a way to help artists show their work publicly. juliecowan.com

Lillian Dailey is a student at the University of Vermont, majoring in English and Agroecology.

Robert Bissell, a retired pediatrician living in Western Massachusetts, is the author of two books, *Best Beloved*, a novel set in New England during the World War1 era, and *Stock Market: You Can Do It*, which details a plan for stock market investments.

Barbara Walter Hetler—mother and grandmother—is the author of two books for readers young and old, *Wand Hill* and *Once in Ordinary Time*.

Jenny Klein is a Wilmette (IL) Public Library Adult Services Librarian. When not behind the Reference Desk, she journals and illustrates each entry, practices yoga or tai chi, reads or listens to books and accompanies her Catahoula, Nelly, on long walks early morning and beach strolls in the afternoon.

Dennis Baron—who has been practicing law in his hometown of Kankakee for 47 years and recently retired from 32 years on the City Council—walks a lot and takes a lot of pictures.

Lisa Hart is a visual artist who finds inspiration in the study of color and nature. She lives in Asheville, North Carolina, with her husband Danny and her poodle Henri.

Keir Graff's fifteen books include suspense novels for adults, adventure tales for kids, and one work of nonfiction. He shares short essays in "Graff Paper," a monthly newsletter available at keirgraff.com/newsletter.

Marylou DiPietro's work has been published in numerous literary magazines and anthologies. Her plays have been produced or developed in Boston, New York City, San Francisco, Los Angeles and London. www.maryloudipietro.com

George Kovac, a Chicago native, is a lawyer in Miami. As a side gig, he edits the "Good Word" of the day column at alphadictionary.com. George keeps up-to-date photos of his sons on his nightstand.

Marilyn Kochman is a writer/editor who lives in central New Jersey.

Chuck Frank lives with his wife, Debbie, in Northbrook, IL.

Patricia Adelstein is retired from the Federal government. She lives on Capitol Hill in Washington, DC, with her husband, Jay.

Chuck Brown lives in Omaha with his wife Danielle, sons Dylan and Nathan, and dog Zoey. He goes by "Chuck" because he got tired of explaining why his parents named him Charlie Brown ... the Third.

Nan Doyal lives in Vermont and is a writer and author of Dig Where You Are, *how one person's effort can save a life, empower a community and create meaningful change in the world.* http://digwhereyouare.com

Manny Brown—who was born in Chicago and went to high school, undergraduate, and graduate school there—is a businessman who grew up near Wrigley and the Cubs, but has always been a White Sox fan.

Nancy Hepner Goodman is a retired Director of Pharmaceutical Research and registered nurse. She writes creative nonfiction and poetry, as she considers the clutter of her storied stuff

Storied Stuff

Mary Loretta Kelly is a retired English teacher, writer, editor, and traveler now left with one student in her life, and a five-year-old grandson with a cracker imagination.

N. G. Haiduck's first book, Cabbie: True Tales, about her experiences driving a cab in New York City in the 1970s, was published by Finishing Line Press (https://www.finishinglinepress.com/product/cabbie-new-york-city-19711972-true-tales-by-n-g-haiduck/.) She and her husband, Neal, recently moved from The Bronx to Burlington, VT.

Peggy Heitmann, a word and visual artist, is an award-winning poet who received a 2024 Pushcart nomination from *Gyroscope Review*. Peggy who lives in Raleigh, NC, with her husband and their two cats, has published poems in, *Gyroscope Review, Wild Word Poetry Remington Review and Atlanta Review.*

Candice Glicken, a retired high school English teacher, is an avid photographer, canasta player, and Edgar, the Shih Tzu lover. She is also president of Eastoncentral.org, which publishes a journal of original poetry, prose and most forms of visual arts.

Pam Gassel is happily retired and enjoying finally being able to relax/hang out with family plus friends after an advertising sales career at the Chicago Tribune for 43 years.

Elaine Johnson, a retired journalist, now spends her time reading, binge-watching all the series she missed and writing whatever she wants. Some of it will soon appear in her Substack newsletter, The End of Everything.

Joni Blecher is a writer and editor living in Portland, Oregon.

Contributor Biographies

Mary B. Hansen is a writer and archivist who understands the power of stories and information to transform lives, including her own. Mary writes personal essays and fiction related to archives and public records from her home in Portland, Oregon. www.marybhansen.com

Susan Grout is an enthusiastic participant in life, lovingly blessed with a great family and happily retired from many years as a psychotherapist.

Kathy Brant taught English and art and then worked many years as a guidance counselor from high school District 99 (Downers Grove, IL). Now retired, she paints needlepoint canvases part-time and enjoys her children, grandchildren and great-grandchildren.

William Anthony, a Senior Lecturer Emeritus of German at Northwestern University, is a writer and painter who lives in Evanston, Illinois, and Edgecomb, Maine. He is the author of the novel *Farnsy* (2022), the story of a good cop on the Maine coast.

Liza Blue is a humor writer. Her work can be found on Substack at lizabluehumorist.substack.com.

Lynn Bodnar is the author of *The Perfect Cupcake, a Momoir*, lives in Colorado, enjoys baking, pondering, and providing energy healing. ecodewithlynn.com

Pat Hitchens is intrigued by all sorts of stuff—storied and not—and her writing has appeared in magazines, on the radio and the Internet. Just to set herself off from the crowd, she's also writing a memoir.

Pat Kreger is a retired television journalist living in Boston.

Keith Kretchmer writes haiku when he's not manufacturing field portable x-ray equipment, taking classes, playing music, or enjoying the views from his home.

Thomas G. Fiffer is co-founder of Christmas Lake Creative, Publisher at Christmas Lake Press, and Partner and Literary Agent at Christmas Lake Literary.

Laurie Kahn, MA, LCPC, MFA, is the Founder of Womencare Counseling and Training Center. She is the author of *Baffled by Love: Stories of the Lasting Impact of Childhood Trauma Inflicted by Loved Ones* (She Writes Press) https://womencarecounseling.com/our-mission/our-perspectives/

Tuni Deignan is an award-winning author, retired dancer, and the mother of five children.

Annette Gendler writes the Substack *The Past and the Present* and is the author of the guide *How to Write Compelling Stories from Family History*, the children's book *Natalie and the Nazi Soldiers*, and the memoir *Jumping Over Shadows*. Visit her at annettegendler.com.

Joanna Clapps Herman has published over fifty pieces since 2020—including poems, short stories, micro fiction, and essays. Book length publications include: *When I am Italian: Quando sono italiana, No Longer and Not Yet: Stories, The Anarchist Bastard: Growing Up Italian in America,* and two edited anthologies: *Wild Dreams* and *Our Roots Are Deep with Passion*. joannaclappsherman.com

Mark Larson is an oral historian and author of *Ensemble: An Oral History of Chicago Theater* and *Working in the 21st Century: An Oral History of American Work in a Time of Economic and Social Transformation.*

Contributor Biographies

Kathleen Caprario-Ulrich traded the concrete canyons of New York City and her home state of New Jersey for the broad skies of Oregon's Willamette Valley, where she writes and is an award-winning visual artist, art educator and occasional stand-up comic.

Ina Chadwick, who lives in Westport, CT, is a lifelong storyteller and founder of achronicles.org, a safe space to share difficult conversations regarding abortion using theater and storytelling.

Suzanne Guess, a writer living in central Iowa where her family has resided for six generations, has an MA from Iowa State University, and an MFA from the University of Nebraska. She recently bought a fancy (expensive) new flute.

Judy Iacuzzi is a retired marketing director and association executive who has authored several published pieces of nonfiction and is redrafting a novel set in Sicily.

Lisa Lauren is a singer-songwriter, pianist, and recording artist living in Evanston, IL. While she never recorded with James Brown, Grammy award-winning sax player David Sanborn is featured on three of her CDs. www.lisalauren.com

Fred Karger is a political consultant, LGBTQ activist, author and adventure seeker who made history as the first openly gay major-party candidate to run for president in 2012. He is the author of two memoirs, one with Steve Fiffer, *Fred Who?*, and one with Sam Eichner, *World's Greatest Crasher*.

Valerie Kretchmer is a recently retired urban planning and real estate consultant. She is a native New Yorker, but happy resident of Evanston, IL.

Fred Gants is a retired management labor and employment lawyer living in Madison, Wisconsin, who admired Marvin Miller, the union business agent who organized major league baseball.

Bob Kaufman is a Chicago attorney with Fischel|Kahn, who likes his olives stuffed with blue cheese.

Robert J. Elisberg is a two-time recipient of the Lucille Ball Award for comedy screenwriting, and as a lyricist is a member of ASCAP. He's written for film, TV, the stage, two novels, political commentary for the *Huffington Post*, and a tech column for the Writers Guild of America.

Allyson Dykhuizen teaches virtual and in-person knitting classes and hosts knitting retreats and events at allysondykhuizen.com.

Josh Kaplan is a former social worker and real estate broker (surprisingly similar careers) who enjoys retirement in Minneapolis, MN, doing some volunteer work, taking long walks and bike rides along the Mississippi River and caring for his Christmas cactus.

Betsy Lackey is a pianist and composer of symphonies inspired by children's stories; one who teaches her students that every time we perform any type of music we are telling a story.

Elizabeth Drucker lives in the suburbs of Chicago and is an MFA student in writing at the University of Nebraska Omaha.

Jean Harned Boyle has lived and worked in four time zones and is now happily retired and living on the beautiful Salish Sea with her husband and dogs—the journey continues.

Abigail Brooks is a senior at the University of Vermont, where she is studying to be an elementary school teacher. She enjoys reading and writing in her free time.

Contributor Biographies

Jim Dodds moved to Vermont in 1967, and married Judy in 1972... lost her to Alzheimer's in May 2020 and started taking his writing and art more seriously again. His artwork can be seen at https://www.youtube.com/watch?v=6e8qXKMe5qk%E2%80%8B.

Bill Durden is President Emeritus, Dickinson College, and a Visiting Scholar, School of Education, Johns Hopkins University.

Robert Jordan, Diplomat in Residence at Southern Methodist University, served as U.S. Ambassador to Saudi Arabia from 2001 to 2003, and is the author, with Steve Fiffer, of *Desert Diplomat: Inside Saudi Arabia Following 9/11*, published by Potomac Books. He is also a contributing columnist for the *Dallas Morning News*.

Mike Conklin is a career journalist who spent 35-plus years in varied roles at the *Chicago Tribune* before leaving to teach and help co-found DePaul University's journalism department. He has written four novels in retirement.

Sally deVincentis *is a retired CEO, writer, and golf professional.*

Larry Cohan is Asst. Professor of Pediatrics at Harvard Medical School. Now retired from Pediatric Care, he continues to teach at Harvard Med, precepting first year students in interviewing skills.

Becca Taylor Gay grew up in Evanston IL, but after retiring from the Design & Production Department of Loyola Press in 2018, transplanted herself to Macon, GA, to enjoy grandchildren and gardening full time.

Patricia Merritt Lear is the author of the short story collection, *Stardust, 7-Eleven, Route 57 and So Forth* (Knopf), and teaches in the MFA in writing program at the University of Nebraska.

Bobbie Calhoun, whose debut novel, *Folio*, was published in March 2025, is a playwright, essayist, poet and novelist. Her work may be found online in *Talking Writing* Literary Journal, Medium, and Storied Stuff, and she has published a book of poetry through Belgrave House.

Jim Cunningham plays guitar and writes songs during retirement.

Peggy Wagner Kimble—after decades living on the east and west coasts—moved back to the town where she wrote this diary.

Sue Gano enjoys writing Flash Non-Fiction. She does her best thinking paddling a kayak on the beautiful Willamette River.

Carol Kanter's poetry has appeared in over ninety literary journals and anthologies and three chapbooks: *Out of Southern Africa*, *Chronicle of Dog*, and *Of Water*. Carol and her photographer husband have paired poems and photographs from their travels in four coffee-table type books: www.DualArtsPress.com

Paula Beardell Krieg learns, creates and teaches, keeping in mind that the best way to do all three is to remember to play.

Christine Goodwin is a retired tax accountant, baker, and knitting enthusiast.

Barbara Huffman's creative writing career began in 2020 when she debuted in the Evanston Public Library digital magazine "10th Ward Lit." She recently published *An Odd Thing Happened*, available on Amazon in both paperback and eBook formats. barbaralandishuffman.com

Mary Campbell is a retired editor who hugs trees.

Bonny Howe, 51, has been an elementary school teacher for 29 years. She treasures nostalgia and precious memories.

Judy Frank Frohlich, though a native Chicagoan, currently lives in Lafayette, California.

Karen Fulks retired as COVID hit, but she is still known as Organizer Extraordinaire. After helping hundreds of people organize their closets, attics, garages and pet areas, she is now organizing her own life and writing about her past.

Reed Ide is a retired writer and editor whose career spanned newspapers, magazines, collectibles, history, and travel.

Lester Jacobson is an award-winning journalist and the author of several short stories and novels. He edits copy and writes columns for the *Evanston RoundTable*.

Melissa Hunt is a writer/screenwriter living in San Francisco with her husband, Dan, and two beagles. When she's not writing, she loves to walk on the beach, drink boba, and keep track of her adult children, Anna and Shamus.

Jean Diamond, a retired CPA, mother of two, grandmother of three, lives with her husband in a suburb of Chicago.

David Inlander has been a practicing attorney and mediator in Chicago for 50 years, and honored to be the Commissioner of FFL CHICAGO, a preeminent fantasy football league for 44 seasons.

Ken Hersh is President & CEO of the George W. Bush Presidential Center, based in Dallas, Texas, and author of *The Fastest Tortoise: Winning in Industries I Knew Nothing About.*

Linda Gartz is a multiple Emmy Award winner for her documentary productions and the author of *Redlined: A Memoir of Race, Change, and Fractured Community in 1960s Chicago,* winner of ten awards, including the Chicago Writer's Association's Indie Nonfiction Book of 2018. The book was named a *Kirkus Reviews* Best Indie Book of 2018.

Sharon Fiffer co-founder of Storied Stuff, has written eight Jane Wheel mysteries (St. Martins/Minotaur), written and edited short fiction and nonfiction, but mostly she knits.

Steve Fiffer, the other Storied Stuff co-founder, is the author of more than twenty books, including his memoir, *Three Quarters, Two Dimes, and a Nickel.*

Made in the USA
Monee, IL
24 June 2025